UNIQUE START UP EXPERIENCE
Raymond J Gonsalves

Story of Larsen and Toubro Ltd,
since inception.
New& revised edition

SYNOPSIS

1936 After winning the contract, for three new cement plants, to be built in India from Tata group, worth 650,000 pounds, a huge sum those days, Larsen returned to Denmark and found Nazis rule it and Hitler needs them. Academic people are frightened and are leaving or have left it.

1938 Larsen is in Bombay again. The idea of setting up L&T came during exile.
"Look at the watch, John." Larsen often commented. "Time is limited." John did not reply, when he left, assured himself. "I am ahead of that watch in my performance."
During this time of war and uncertainty, Larsen and Toubro conceived a dream and believed, "better times will come."

They told same thing to William Bendictson and John A Gonsalves to have faith and hold on.

"With sincere determination anything is possible."

Preface

"What was it like, during the early days of L&T?" An article was titled and printed in Powai pageant in early seventies and it continued." None is better qualified to answer this question than a draftsman in Architectural dept."

John A Gonsalves was the first drawing office staff member recruited by L&T partnership, a joint decision of William Bendictson, H.H. Larsen and S.K.Toubro in1942. He had not only the opportunity to work with the founders of L&T but also the chance to rub shoulders with them.

Initially L& T rented one room with one table space only, when professionals just peeped into it and left, John took the risk, joined this small firm which was struggling to survive, for he recognized their potential and had faith in them.

"In service lies success."

This story of L&T, is a unique Start Up experience, how two technically educated persons take refuge in Bombay and make a new beginning in life. How John came in contact with L&T and the tipping point that changed their life. It is based on true life experience of John with L&T, reveals other side of the coin, never told before, as related by him to his son Raymond.

What compelled H.H.Larsen and S.K. Toubro to give up their native Denmark ?

Take refuge in Bombay and make a new beginning here?

To answer this question, it is necessary to read the history of Europe between 1930 to 1945.

1930

Depression in USA, affected Europe also, with high inflation and vast unemployment, the situation became worse in countries like Germany, Denmark, it gave chance for a lair and cruel person like Hitler, came to power, to fulfil his ambition of conquering the whole of Europe, he compelled many Germans and Danish persons, sent them to fight on many fronts.

So, they escaped, to take refuge elsewhere, some went to West, others came to Bombay and thought and hoped, the war will end soon, when the situation in Europe will improve, and they will be able return home.

But that was not case, this war compelled many people to stay back in Bombay, as it was safe and far from actual fighting.

It was during (Larsen&Toubro's) exile in Bombay, an idea of setting up a new company came to their mind. On 1 May1938 with very limited means, they rented one room that had space to fit one table only, to start as consultants, specialized in setting up a complete new modern cement plant.

It's war time and business men are afraid and not interested in setting up any new business. Consultants get no business in their line of specialization.

Next it started import of dairy products and machinery and supplied it to British army.

1941/42 German U boats sink Allied merchant ships and air force pounds London, Britain is isolated and imports of dairy products and machinery stops.

Without space for design room, fabrication and finishing workshop, L&T thinks of import substitutions, it put an advertisement for a draftsman, thirty men responded and stood in line for it, only one John A Gonsalves a supervisor of Royal navy ship repair workshop is selected.

"I do not know what inspired me to go for that interview, twenty-six men stood in line for it, and two European stood near the door, I thought they had also come for this interview. When I came close and saw one old man is seated inside, questioning a candidate. Second interview, same two men who stood outside, introduce themselves to me, as founders of this partnership firm." John commented.

1944 The Bombay dock fire had burnt down most of business areas surrounding the dock. L&T's rented two rooms, one at Calicut Street, Fort and another at Nicol street, Ballard estate in Bombay, both went up in smoke and were not traceable. John HMS naval workshop was still in the same place in the dock. Where was L&T and its name plate?

In many profiles of Henning H Larsen and Soren K Toubro, written by different persons, many facts are omitted. Even the name of third partner William Bendictson is not mentioned, and the role played by John A Gonsalves is forgotten or ignored. But without the help from these two men, would L&T ever see the morning sunrise again?

It was their hard work and devotion that pumped new blood into veins of a sick child called L&T and showed it how to walk.

Then when L&T was well established and making profits, many empty suits joined the company, have written Big stories about their contributions, ideas, in making this one table space company great, leaving the real soldiers aside. I leave it to you the reader, first read this story and then give your judgement.

Dedication

Devoted to the memory of John A Gonsalves, a humble, optimistic man, worked devotionally without reacting to outcome of the work, he contributed his ideas and showed a crawling baby how to stand on its legs.

To understand story of L&T, a reader should know Brief history of Europe between 1930 to 1945.

Chapter no 1

Japan

Nineteen century Japan was not a developed country, in 1868 Emperor Meiji wrote a slogan "a prosperous nation, strong army." To achieve his goal, he made education compulsory for all, sent young Japanese men to USA, England and Germany, to study science and western techniques of manufacture; especially iron and steel works, railways, shipyards and other modern industries. He also hired foreign experts and technicians to train local workforce in these essential modern skills. After they had acquired these facts and skills, they modernized Japan and the Japanese economy grew and the nation became strong and prosperous. Emperor Meiji also built a physically powerful army and navy, that by start of twentieth century, Japan was in commanding position, enough to face USA and Europe on equal terms. Japan defeated Russia in1905.

1920

The land mass of USA is huge and most of it is fertile land. It grows many types of grains, fruits and vegetables and nuts, same land is also rich in natural resources like gold, oil to run engines, water and coal to generate electricity, iron ore to make steel etc. Another advantage USA has, its population density is less compared its land area. It has good education facilities and technical training institutes, which has educated and skilled its people, made them intelligent and research centers help them innovative. Wright brothers invented first aircraft, Henry Ford made model T cars and he also established factory assembly line system to mass produce the same. Business men in USA built many factories to manufacture vast quantity of consumers goods like cars, refrigerators, radios, and other electric items etc, and it exported cars, aircrafts other items to many countries. As businesses prospered and profits increased, people were paid better wages.

USA -1928

A new President Herbert Hoover took office, assured

the people, USA will become prosperous and advance nation, poverty would disappear soon and it will become history. He believed if the government took care business men's well-being, offered them better incentives, everyone will flourish. Industrialists will start new businesses and will built more factories, employ more workers and pay better wages. He belonged to Republican Party and he confidently told Americans, there would soon be, "a chicken in every pot and two cars in every garage." His government imposed high import duties on goods imported from aboard, reduced taxes on goods made in USA. Income tax was also reduced on business profits, so businessmen saved lot of money and reinvested it in other industries. The capitalist was already wealthy and with more business income, rich became richer, as large income from businesses remained with them.

With new era of prosperity, the profits of the companies grew, so was the people's urge to buy shares of the companies "on the margin," became a sort of fever on the Wall Street that there were street fights among brokers, share prices also touched the sky. The expanded industries of USA started producing more and more, all types of goods, greater than what people could consume, so the supply side exceed the demand.

 The reality was different, the real consumers were workers and farmers who did not have money to buy the extra produce, as wealth was concentrated in the hands of few businessmen. So, the surplus production remained unsold and profits of companies fell.

After much speculation on the stock market, when the investors and public became aware of results of banks and companies, they authorized their brokers to dumped millions and millions of shares, they had purchased earlier, the share prices fell and the bubble busted.

 Wall Street Crashed on 24th October1929 thousands of banks and companies closed down, and prosperity in USA ended.

When the old good days ended, poverty and unemployment returned to USA which led to great depression of 1930.

It affected trade with Europe and Japan also.

The Versailles treaty

The Allied countries (England, France and Russia) defeat Germany in First World War which ended on

11 November 1918. In May 1919 the Allied leaders drafted a peace treaty called the Versailles treaty and compelled Germany to sign it, which was one sided and unfair, as it took away lot of land from it. Germany was also duty-bound to possess a small army, small navy without sub marines and no air force. Since this war was fought on French soil, it also paid war damages to France.

The Germans understood this treaty was accepted on wrong terms and conditions by Weimar government, they hated this government for signing it and wanted to change it. For Germans it was a discrimination. 1930 depression affected Germany, due to slump in business activities, there was high inflation and soaring unemployment. Trade with other countries decreased and its currency became so worthless that small shopkeepers issued vouchers to their employees instead of German mark.

People were frustrated with the government, many felt it had failed in duty to protect common man from unemployment and inflation.

The Germans desired a change in government, but were not sure who is better, communism or Nazis? Small traders and businessmen feared, if the communist came to power, they would lose their right to property, all means of production would be owned by the government.

 Adolf Hitler, a painter and then became soldier, later National socialist party leader. He understood what people wanted, to take revenge on Weimar government for accepting the unfair and one-sided Versailles Treaty. In his election campaign, he promised jobs to the German people, and when in power not to honor the Versailles treaty, thus to destroy the present government, restore back Germany to its former glory.

 He also promised the people, he will not pay any compensation to France and win back the lands taken from Germany.

In 1933 Hitler's Nazi party came to power, he banned all rival political parties, imprisoned their leaders and close down newspapers. He took away the worker's right to strike and stopped all unions activities. He setup a secret police force called Gestapo to spy on others, now Hitler spies were everywhere in factories, shops, colleges, even in schools. Anyone spoke against Hitler or Nazis was arrested. He ordered all young men must serve the army for certain period of time.

Hitler ordered Nazis to beat the socialists,

communist and supporters of rival parties. He was a suspicious, rude and cold-blooded man, if he doubted a person; he would finish him.

SA leader Ernest Roehm had played important role in bring Hitler to power, was ambitious man and had formed a new army to take over Germany, but when Hitler came to know about this, he turned against him, on the "Night of long knives" he dragged him and his supporters out from their beds and murdered them. Now there was no opposition left in Germany.

 Since Hitler hated the Jews, he took away all their rights and their means of earning a livelihood like groceries shops, bakeries pharmacies, butcheries etc were all taken over, they were also prohibited from taking up any government jobs. He was spreading lies about Jews and communists, told people they were responsible for Germany's problems. He burnt Jews synagogues and smashed their houses. It was a crime to be Jew in Germany.

The second Exodus started, Jews fled to save their lives, some escaped from Germany to the west but millions were trapped and pushed into concentration camps where they were later murdered in cold blood.

1935. The ghost of the 1st World War still haunts Germany, not only for defeat but also for loss of lands and prestige. Hitler is clever and knows what to do for his country to regain its glory. He builds and strength Germany's industrial base, economy improves and unemployment decreases, Germans are pleased they have work. At the same time Hitler employs more men, expands and strength the army, navy and air force. He also knew why Germany lost the 1st World War, "the only new weapon was the battle tank invented by Britain which made the difference on the battle field."

He builds new and better tanks for the army, modern ships for navy and new aircrafts for air force. Since people find work, they put faith in Hitler and recognized him, as a new great leader, a miracle maker for the German people. Industrial production increases and inflation decreases, German mark appreciates.

"As to his popularity, especially among the youth of Germany, there can be no manner of doubt. The old trust him, young idolize him. It is the worship of national hero that saved his country from all her oppressors. "Thomas Man a great German writer remarked.

To fulfill his election promises, Hitler invades Poland and regains the land taken from Germany; then took Rhineland north of France rich in iron and coal. So, for people Hitler is a man who stands by his words, people and army put great faith in him.

Now military service is compulsory, young men are forced to join the war.

Chapter no 2
Two school friends

The depression of 1930 not only affected Germany but Denmark also, the situation was similar, there was high inflation, large scale unemployment plus shortages of many essential items.

 Soren K.Toubro was born on 27 February 1906 in Denmark, information about his parents is not known, except he completed his schooling from Jesuit school in Copenhagen and then finished his civil engineering degree from Technical University of Denmark. He joined F L Smidth &Co as sales engineer, where he studied the technique of constructing a new cement plant from its inception and was trained in many aspects of commissioning it.

1934 This company was a world leader in cement plant technology, it was engaged in designing cement plants, plus manufacturing of equipment and spares for it, provided consultancy service and sold products worldwide. In Sindh province of India, the Rohri cement factory, it had already designed, supplied equipment, built, and commissioned it. So, it maintained a branch office at Eros building; opposite Churchgate station in Bombay to serve more Indian clients. This branch office took care of its business interest in the Indian sub-continent.

It sent S K Toubro a civil engineer, as a consultant to build and commission the Madukkarai Cement works at Coimbatore in Madras province, where he lived and worked for four years.

Henning Holck Larsen was born on July 4 1907 in Copenhagen, Denmark and was the only son of Louis Holger Larsen and Ida Jorgensen. He and Toubro went to same Jesuit primary and secondary school in Copenhagen and became closely acquainted, after they had completed their schooling both still maintained their close association with each other.

Larsen graduated from University of Copenhagen in Arts in 1925. He secured a job of a cement chemist with F.L. Smidth & Co. while working with this company, he was given the opportunity to study further, so he completed his thesis for Master of Science in chemical engineering from Royal School of Polytechnics in 1930.

His father Louis worked as stationmaster for the Danish railways, which he left it later and went to South Africa, where he joined the South African Railway construction company and he lived there for many years. He was involved in Boer War and for his bravery he earned two medals. After the war he returned to Denmark.

Since his childhood, Larsen was fascinated by natural beauty of our planet, so he wanted to travel and see many places. He had studied geography of the world thoroughly and was familiar with the maps of the world, so he loved adventure. He had already travelled to Sweden, Norway, Germany and Austria with his parents. This developed the spirit of quest in him, his thirst to travel and see other parts of the world remained. His favorite subjects were mathematics, physics, and chemistry.

F.L. Smidth &Co was engaged in designing, manufacturing equipment and supplying cement plants worldwide, Larsen studied and mastered the art and science of designing new cement plants and equipment. When he had acquired thorough know how about it, he insisted with management of the company that they should send him out soon, as sales engineer to different parts of the world, for since his childhood he longed to travel and see the beauty of many different parts of the world.

After he had finished his training and when company was confident about his ability in sales, it sent him first to Poland as sales consultant to sell cement plant technology and equipment, next he was sent to Middle East, Egypt, Syria, and Lebanon. Later he also went to Iraq and Iran, he brought in good new business.

The evolution of different species of birds and animals, on the island of Madagascar, separated from main land Africa, captivated his imagination so as tourist he also visited it.

In 1935, Tata group wanted to set up some new cement plants with the latest Danish technology and equipment, it was in touch with F. L. Smidth &Co

through its branch office at Bombay. To finalize this proposal, it invited the representatives of this company to Bombay. The chairman is aware; Larsen has thorough knowledge of setting up new cement plants and is systematic in his consultancy job with better ability in sales. In December 1935 chairman instructed Larsen to do the costing of three new plants and prepare a quotation for the client i.e. landed cost at Bombay. Then he sent him to Bombay, to consult and fix this deal.

In Bombay, meetings were arranged between the directors of the Tata group and Larsen, the discussions and negotiations went on for many days. During these meetings, many queries were raised by the client, on different aspects of setting up a new cement plant with best technology, costing and time of completion. Larsen gave most convincing explanations about the advance Danish technology, design, finance, period of completion of the new plant. Most of the debate was between Larsen and the directors of Tata group. So, the client was surprise, sales engineer had better knowledge and experience. It was also pleased with the consultant's advice, so they accepted his suggestion on merger of eight different cement plants into one group, which resulted in the formation of Associated Cement Company (ACC).

This negotiation resulted in a confirmed order for three new cement plants to be built in India, the contract was worth 650,000 pounds, a very huge sum those days that none of the directors of Tata group were willing to sign it. This contract papers was left with the chairman to sign it.

This compelled chairman of F. L. Smith &Co to travel to Bombay as this contract was to be signed between chairmen of two different companies.

The chairman of F. L. Smith &Co is pleased that his firm has succeeded in winning this big contract, he travels to Bombay.

 When meets Larsen, instead of appreciation and reward for his efforts, the chairman speaks in terms of money and ignores hard work, his technical knowledge, his efforts in persuasive of this contract. When this deal was about to be signed, he remarked.

" Never in your life, will you see such a big contract signed."

Larsen was surprised to hear this funny statement but he remained calm. The chairman instead of raising Larsen's standard of performance and praising his efforts or congratulating him or promising him monetary reward. He acted different, not as per Larsen's expectations, he did not like such behavior from this chairman. He was disappointed, soon realized that he was main man who convinced clients and helped the company to win big orders. He had more capabilities in sales, business development, and better engineering knowledge in convincing new clients. The chairman is less experience in the same field, who only boasts to him about his influence and ability to sign large contracts, worth lakhs of pounds. Whenever this recollection came to his mind, he had a big laugh.

During his stay in Bombay, Larsen roams and studies the place, he finds the cotton mills and other auxiliary industries, thinks India is still a virgin country, it lacks basic industries like iron and steel, cement, dairy plants etc. He thinks India is underdeveloped country but it is the best city in the East with 24 hours of water and electricity.

1936 Germany invades and occupies Denmark, British occupy Iceland a Danish's colony.
1936 February, Larsen returns to Denmark, staggered to see Danes are ruled by Nazis. He finds the situation in Denmark has become worse, there is

huge unemployment and high inflation, there is rationing of food and other essential items, shortage of petroleum products and the economy has deteriorated. Hitler's ambition of conquering whole of Europe has spoiled the show, many Danish exports items meant for other counties are diverted to Germany.

F.L.Smidth & co with the biggest order in hand from Tata group, worth 650000 pounds for three cement plants, which is on drawing board, is not allowed to export cement plant technology plus equipment to India. Germany needs them, company is compelled to divert these plants to Germany, Larsen efforts in winning and convincing client, the Tata contract is ruined.

The League of nations which promised to settle disputes without the use of arms or wars, has remained a promise on paper, Italy and Japan both walked of it, and joined hands with Germany. These three members states, gloried war and idea of superior race, fit to rule the inferior nations and race.

By 1936 Hitler turns the table on allied countries by signing Rome Berlin Axis agreement with Mussolini, Japan also joins it in 1937.

King Christian X of Denmark finds Hitler rules his country and does not recognize the 1920 borders of Denmark, he is helpless and powerless, he rides his own horse without a guard.

Denmark is a per pet in the hands of Nazis, the relationship between Germany and Britain is damaged, the communication between India under British rule and Denmark is prohibited. So F.L. Smidths is helpless and cannot communicate or execute the orders of Tata group for three cement plants, Denmark can only produce goods Germany needs, many type products are diverted to it.

At home Larsen is frustrated, all his efforts and hard work in wining this biggest contract for the company are in vain.

Hitler's rule has frightened people, made them obedient and fanatic. To fulfill his ambition of conquering whole of Europe, military service is compulsory. He is utilizing services of young educated men, for waging a war against other nations. Larsen is in Denmark, notes these changes taking place in Europe.

"What will happen to my technical qualification? Where will Hitler utilize my talent?" Next, he visualizes.

Many questions come and filter through his mind, he realized that Nazis will compel him to become a soldier, send him to the front to fight. He does not want to join the army and waste his talent for this mad man.

"Bombay India is better and safer place to be, I had been there before, and my best friend Toubro is in India also, I will to stay there, till the war is over." He consoles himself.

 So, he decided to leave his native place and settle elsewhere, He left Denmark for India.

Chapter no 3

Unusual situation

In 1938 Hitler invades and occupies the Austrian empire which comprises of many countries like

Austria, Serbia, Bosnia and then occupies Czechoslovakia. He threatens Britain and France, and starts the Second World War.

Hitler makes military service compulsory; more young men are sent to fight on many fronts. The world is at war and the situation in Denmark is getting worse.

1938 Larsen left Denmark and is in Bombay, India again, he corresponds with Toubro and warns him that Nazis control Denmark and there is no free press, they don't listen to our people, there is turmoil in Europe that going back home is risky.

"If we go back home, we might get involved with the war or sent to the front to fight and all our knowledge will blow up like a cigarette's smoke." Larsen cautions him.

Through correspondence, he seriously convinces his friend to stay back here, till the war ends. He requests Toubro when you are in Bombay, we will meet and discuss the situation further, what next step to take, whether to stay safe here or return back home, I am watching the state of affairs in Europe, will it improve? What option left, if we cannot go back, also of making a new beginning here, he thinks of starting up a new company.

When Toubro was released from his assignment at Coimbatore in Madras province, they met in Bombay and found it is a trend among the people to spend the summer at a pleasant place. Not accustomed to the hot and humid climate of the coast, they went to Matheran, a hill station closes to Bombay, to spend some days there.

Larsen advises Toubro. "After winning such a big contract from Tatas for three new cement plants, worth lakhs of pounds, the company cannot execute it, all my efforts loss, our exports are diverted by Nazis to Germany," he said,

"Nazis rule Denmark, what option left with us, is to go back, join mad Hitler in war and die. Second we start a new firm of our own here and prosper."

"The world war is on, traveling back home is also not safe." He adds.

Toubro agrees "I understand, Japan expanding in east and Hitler in west, better to take refuge here."

Larsen is able to convince Toubro, "India being an under develop nation, offers marvelous opportunities in line of our expertise, we can set up a new consulting firm, offer engineering consultancy services for assembling and commissioning of new cement, dairy plants so on."

They are aware, in India there are very few cement plants and there is huge shortage of cement, it offers vast scope for qualified personnel like him and Toubro, with experience in establishment of new cement plants, we can make a new beginning here. He properly visualized a dream that there is tremendous scope for their talent, they will procure new orders and execute them. Not only it would benefit them and make them well-off, India will also get the basic material for its progress and India's image will change, from backward to progressive country.

" So, we can (Larsen&Toubro) established a new partnership firm, as consultants with expertise in cement and dairy plants,"

L&T thinking, there is great demand here.

Later we will diversify into other businesses and then bring in new advance European technology to manufacture other products. Larsen had already conveyed his ideas to his school friend Toubro through letters, who was working as a consultant at Coimbatore in Madras province, on deputation from the same company F.L. Smidth& co.

After graduation in different fields, they were lucky to get the opportunity to work for the same company, so their friendship continued, grew and became stronger. They trusted each other and always kept in touch through correspondence, often exchange views and ideas to know the other person's opinion.

"Also, Hitler is ruthless killer, has already killed many opposition leaders, communists and the Jews; he does not tolerate any criticism or opposition." Larsen added.

Toubro is also aware of what's happening in the world especially Europe.

Larsen said "Why have many Danish people taken refuge here?"

They both agreed to stay back, so they thoroughly discussed the scope and other aspect of this new business, they are about to commence.

The war in Europe compelled them to think twice, whether return to Denmark or not? they better wait for situation to recover, and peace to be restored. They thought.

Peace in Europe, for these displaced men was illusive, as more countries came under Hitler 's control, it built a strong desire to be safe here, and venture on own, be independent.

"We can also approach Tata group and assure them we can execute old contract, to build three new cement plants for them, which the firm F.L. Smidth& co in Denmark had contracted to execute." Larsen suggested.

They discuss among themselves.

"What about the design drawings, plant and machinery? will Tata group listen to us?" Toubro replied.

"I think, No," Larsen replied.

Denmark is in war zone, what is better, than to be safe here, at present we live in India now, they thought.

Both visited F.L. Smidth &co, branch office at Churchgate Bombay, they informed the staff, that they are staying back, in Bombay till the war ends.

To make a new beginning and be independent, they formed partnership firm, called Larsen and Toubro private ltd on 1 May 1938 and rented a small room that had space for one table only, at Calicut street, fort, Bombay.

L&T ventured, with great hopes of getting business in their line of engineering expertise, thinking better times will come, the world is at war, there is fear and distrust in the minds of the people, this created uncertainty, Indian businessmen are more cautious, they think twice before setting up a new business-like cement plants or any other related business. It becomes difficult for this new firm to get business, so there is no cash flow.

By March 1938 Germany captures Poland and much of Europe is under German's control. Japan controls great part of china and Far East.

Exodus

Military service is compulsory in Germany and Denmark. By 1940 Hitler had compelled many technically educated people to join the war, many were fighting on all fronts,

Daily more and more people were getting killed or killing others, witnessing this chaos, the attitude of many young and educated Germans and Danes had changed.

L&T did not believe in wasting their time and talent for Hitler, they thought he is insane. This dictator with full power and no opposition is doing whatever that pleases him. He is leading the Germans and others in wrong direction.

 Brilliant and better educated people like Albert Einstein have deserted Germany. When Denmark came under Nazi's control, same thing was happening there, people escaped, some went to USA and Canada, others came to India. William Benedickson also thought the same and managed to travel from U.K. to Europe; he came to Bombay and joined L&T in 1940.

During this period of world war, though the English accepted Danes in Bombay, they kept watch on those living here, for they suspected them of spying and supporting the Nazis, many Danish suspects were caught and imprisoned in India.

In Europe, it was very frightening, to city after city is getting destroyed by war. Fear and uncertainty have gripped people of the world, people are leaving their businesses and fleeing their homes. Refugees are flooding other nations.

Many Danish and German people had left their countries and settled elsewhere, through these Danish settlers in Bombay Larsen comes in contact with Karen Speyer, they meet, fall in love. He is thirty old, marries her, marriage take place at a church in south Bombay and they settle down here.

 L&T's consultancy business was not doing well, it also represented some Danish dairy products & equipment manufacturers and imported butter, cheese, milk pasteurizers, various mobile milk carriers and dairy machinery and spares from England and Denmark and supplied to the British military.

In 1939, within a year of setting up L&T, Britain declared war on Germany, Hitler sent U boats and blocked the supply routes to U.K. it was isolated. Indian imports and exports were irrupted, hence L&T import business was also stopped due to war. Germany takes over Czechoslovakia and then conquers Poland and Finland. Thus, Hitler showed the Germans that he is a man of word, who makes promises and fulfills them. His great ambition to occupy the whole of Europe and keeping it under his control is achieved.

In 1939 British India, in order to gain support of the Indian people; they released some Indian national leaders from the prisons. British persuade the Congress leaders to support them during the world war. They refused to do so and saw this as an opportunity to weaken the British Empire, more by non-cooperation.

Mahatma Gandhi had already started a civil disobedience (Passive resistance or non-violence movement) called Satyagraha, strikes were common in India people wanted to end British rule. British realized it was difficult to rule India without people's hold.

Subhas Chandra Bose did not believe in Gandhi's philosophy of non-violence and wants to kick the British out; he escaped to Malaya with his supporters and he joined the Japanese army.

In 1940 France surrendered to Germany and other small nations like Holland and Belgium also came under Hitler's control.

1941/42 German U boats rule the Atlantic Ocean and German air force pounds London, cuts off the sea lanes to Britain. Imports of food, essential material for industries has stopped, England is in a desperate state, L&T cash flow depends on imported dairy machinery and products from Europe, it stopped. The survival of this small firm is thorny.

During Second World War, most of fighting was going on the both the sides of the globe, in Europe, Burma and the Fareast. Bombay was far from the action of the real fighting.

During the First World War, India had supplied thousands of men and dispatched huge quantity of material, food through Bombay dock to fight this war. Since this dock had rendered great service to the British army to win this war, British realized the role it played, so in its honor for the great services rendered by this dock in repairs, maintenance of ships and transportation of men material and food to Europe.

 As a tribute for its service and help, they built and erected a concrete stage type memorial at Ballard estate near the dock, it is still standing here, people can visit it and read the statements written on a rectangular copper plate and attached to it, about the services provided by Bombay dock during First World War.

The chapter no 4

Story of John

John A Gonsalves was born on 10th June 1921 at
Bandra and was baptized at St Andrew church. His
father Diego Sabastian Gonsalves, a qualified school
teacher, taught in English medium school at
Andheri, a suburb of Bombay. His mother Mary
Gonsalves was educated up to the six standards from
an English medium school in Vile Parle, Bombay.
At that time, only qualification needed to obtain a
good job in Bombay was a person ability to speak
English. She had extra advantage as she could read,
write and also speaks English fluently. She loved her
independence and as house wife devoted her time
towards her children and house work. She owns
land, so cultivated vegetables in her field and earned
enough money to live a better life. She was tall fair,
often mistaken to be an English woman by the color

of her skin white chocolate type.

Diego left teaching and secured a job of an accounts clerk with British Army and Navy stores in Bombay where he worked up to 1949.

John completed his secondary schooling from St Andrews High School, Bandra and then finished his civil draftsman course from a reputed college in Bombay. He was intelligent man and was fast learner. In 1940 was recruited as trainee supervisor by H.M.S. (His Majesty Service) Naval dockyard at Bombay, his training is less theory and more of practical during the war, it was on the spot survey of damage ships, as more were in waiting for repairs inside the dock as well as floating outside.

Then referring the original drawings, discussing with his team, to find a solution to fix it. His training lasted for a period of one year and he was trained in various trades, concerning repairs of the Royal navy ships, he soon picks up the routine work, especially surveying the damage vessel and referring the original drafts, discussing with his team, a repair plan. When he had completed his course in ship repairing he was handed over the responsibility of managing the naval ship repair work shop at Bombay dock.

1940 India was mostly an agricultural economy, basic education and industries are mostly concentrated in big cities, it produces few engineers and at HMI naval dockyard there were none. So, the workers considered the draftsman to be one, since he performed the main job of first surveying the damaged Royal Navy ships, after that he prepared the action plan. He also guided the workers in executing the repair job.

During both first and second world wars, Bombay dock had served as safe harbor to park Allied ships, away from the battle field, so dock and sea surrounding it, was always overcrowded with all kinds of ships. Most of Royal navy ships which had served many parts of the Indian ocean and other places, needed urgent repairs or servicing, they came here and got their work done. But problem was remained the same, to get a berth inside the dock, even merchant ships faced the same difficulty, waiting time extended by a week or more due to over load. There was no proper control over the work load, so waiting period got mostly extended due to limited capacity. For Royal navy ships the situation had not changed in the Bombay dock during Second World War, even necessary supplies were on hold due to unavailability of berth, and the waiting time to enter dock for service or repairs amplified and created disorder and confusion.

But there were men with courage and will power, who had the patience to hold on, it is they that provided the help and service needed, to make the Royal navy fit, to fight and resist the German and Japanese take over.

During the period of war, motto of the workers. "To keep the tempo of resistance up always, to keep naval ships fit, to beat Germany and Japan navies." "Complicated or simple, the job must be completed without resistance."

It was a time when the work was carried on war footing. Whenever an English Navy captain came to the naval workshop looking for an engineer, he is directed by workers to John, convinced that he understands the English ascent and can handle him properly. He not only understood English ascent but also looked like an English man. John assured the captain that his needs will be taken care of.

There is no time to waste, as the yard is overload with work and the sea is overcrowded with ships. Work is continuously monitored and pressure is applied by superiors, to get the work in hand completed fast.

1941 June 22, Hitler wanted more living space for Germans, started Operation Barbarossa, invades USSR in winter and due to the severe cold climate, Germans tanks, guns, ammunitions and equipment are frozen in icy cold, even soldiers' uniform is not fit for the weather. He orders the German army to halt thirty miles before Moscow.

7th December 1941 Japan bombs American naval base at Pearl Harbor in the Pacific, it conquers Singapore and Malaya and advances into Burma. Hitler controls Europe, and Britain is isolated, tired exhausted. USA joins the war and Lend lease to provide food, guns and aircrafts helps U.K. to hold on.

After Pearl Harbor was damaged by Japan, British became cautious, fears they may attack Madras, Calcutta, and Bombay also. All military camps along the coast line of India are on high alert.

1942. Jinnah demands India should be divided in two parts, on the basis of religion and the Muslims must be given the North West part of India, to create a separate nation state called Pakistan. It is his idea of two nations theory that creates distrust and hatred between Hindus and Muslims, there are communal riots in Bombay and other parts of India. In 1942 Congress launches the Quit India movement at August Kranti ground Grant road in Bombay. John had completed two years of service with the naval workshop, under the control of Royal navy, he was paid well and his job is stable. He was happy, always busy daily performing different types of ship repair jobs and was gaining experience from it. Naval repair workshop was overload with work, in that chaos, it was necessary to have a cool mind, to bear the pressure of work. That's what John had, the patience and perseverance to take on, whatever the workload that came his way and continue, thinking, it's all for the country.

Daily he received the newspaper at home but found less time in the morning to browse it. At the dock, one afternoon while he was browsing the newspaper, an advertisement in the situation vacant column attracted his attention.

"Wanted a draftsman, with experience in civil and mechanical drafting for Danish consultants." Meet personally at the address given below. It was the L&T's first advertisement put for recruitment of a skill personnel.

It was like some external force had inspired John on

the appointment day, to go for this interview, so he excused himself and went in search of this unknown firm.

On 1 May 1938 at Calicut street, fort, L&T had started partnership firm with one table space only room, it was converted into a warehouse. Next it rented another similar room, situated in building at Nicole Street, Ballard estate in Bombay.

At that time, this consultancy firm with Danish name, was like another transport freight agent with one table space only, waiting for business to come. It was not familiar name even in this area, for lack of business, as few people ever interacted with it. So, with whomever John inquired about its name and address, the strangers looked blank and none were able to guide him. As a consultant firm it was mostly without work, so it was not known. Even when he was roaming within its close location, the persons replied "No idea," none were able to guide him, to find this firm.

At last, he concluded; it was useless asking people for the address. He stopped and when he raised his head, he saw a big Q. He declared that was what he had been searching for, he went close and counted, twenty-six men are standing in the Q, in the front of the same building.

 "You have come for an interview, stand behind the last man." Office boy by the name of Frank told him. John waited in the Q for his turn to come; soon he noticed two European men are standing outside near the door of L&T's room, he thinks, they have also come for same interview.

Slowly the Q started to decrease, he came close the room, and peeped inside it, he was astonished to see, the room is very small, can fit only one table inside it. An old European man is seated and interviewing a candidate. Filled with negative thoughts in his mind, he stood near the door.

 "This interview is waste of time, not worth it. Since I have stood in the Q for some time, I better complete this interview." He said to self.

John is summoned in, presents his bio data to William Bendictson, a veteran civil engineer with many years of project experience in civil mechanical electrical works in advance countries of Europe, who comprehends him systematically.

" The interview was a thorough military drill. "John made a remark to his friend.

Back home he received a letter and was called for second interview. John went back to the same place and when he was about to entered L&T's room, two men interrupted, hello him and introduce themselves to him, stating they are the founders of this new partnership firm called "Larsen & Toubro Pvt ltd" named after their surnames. He recollected, they are same two men that stood outside near the door of the firm, at the time of his first interview.

After introduction was over, they took him to a restaurant close by.

"We like know more about your role in the shipyard?" Larsen inquired.

"I am draftsman trained in repairs of Royal navy warships here, we perform all types of jobs required to make the ship refloat, have complete setup of toolroom, fabrication workshop, etc." John replied.

"We are qualified engineers, worked for F. L. Smidth, experience in setting up new cement plants." Larsen began his speech.

 "Many clients have sort and utilized my expertise and knowledge to build complete new cement plants, as sales consultant, I have sold and commissioned many of them throughout Middle East." Larsen explained his working experience.

"Before setting this firm, I was a consultant, I have completed and commissioned new plant at

Coimbatore in Madras province" Toubro said.

Over a cup of tea; these men took their turn to explain their great experiences and also about their new visualized visions of this new firm to John, assuring him that vast opportunities exist in construction of new cement plants in India, also in civil, mechanical and electrical works pertaining to it.

 Larsen spoke again, "It was I, who convinced Tata group and secured the biggest order from them, to build three new cements plants in India, worth six and half lakh pounds."

"An agreement was signed between Tatas and F L Smidth & co." Larsen puts forward the copy of agreement.

John examines the copy and hands it back.

"I understand, you are qualified and experience persons," John replied.

"You want me to joins your firm and work as draftsman, but where is drawing room, where will I do the drafting work?" John inquired.

"Today we have one table space only, but I assure you, have faith in us, you will see our vision materialized, our factories will be laid with hundreds of tables for staff." Larsen boldly replied.

"We assure you a bright future if you join and work for us but ignore the present state of this firm."
William also joins in the debate. Even Toubro supports them.

"Looks like they are dream merchants, hallucinating and selling them to me." John said to self.

"How will this dream materialized without a factory set up?" John inquired.

"We are experienced engineers, rare to find in India today, soon we will have a setup, we assure you trust us."

John understood, these three persons are technically qualified and experience personnel in different fields of engineering. They have a personality to convince people about their ability in executing big projects. Their talks were very substantial which made him believe they are really qualified and experience people. He thinks there is great future for this small firm in India, they are at present unsettled by war, like many other refugees settled in Bombay. They are trying to make a new beginning here and are also trying to convince him, a well settled person working for Royal navy to join them.

These three men observed John personality and found he is tall fair and healthy young boy, with board arms, also looks like a European, he is smart and suitable man. Within seconds both parties judge each other, John takes second look, finds two men in early thirty, have dynamic personality. It was a symptomatic meeting of great minds who immediately understood each other.

From 1938 to 1942, for four years, this firm struggles to get business in their line of engineering expertise, L&T realized there was no much scope left in it, and is incomplete without new projects in hand.

During the Second World War, the sea near dock is over crowded with warships, and merchant ships, that need service and repairs. L&T understood there is had great potential in it, but we do not have expertise in it, fortunately we have at hand William Benedictson an engineer with experience in mechanical projects. Also, John with Royal Navy ship repairing experience, he repairs wars ships.

After hearing about John back ground, experience in naval ship repairs, L&T was convinced, it has the right man at hand, that's what they were looking for, at the time of world war, rare to find such a person. They were always thinking far ahead of their time, dreaming and confident about the future. Even when the present was not so promising, the future looked bright for them.

At that time L&T was managing the show, with one table space room only, there was no space for another person to seat inside this room at the same time. Even when clients visited them, to meet and discuss a proposal, it was one person at a time inside and two stood outside. When there was no space for drawing room, it put an advertisement for a draftsman.

After some days, John received a second hand written letter at home confirming his selection. At first John hesitated to join these three engineers, who were just selling their dreams or offering ideas to please and persuade him to join them.

 Bombay Port was well established, a safe place to serve for long years and get yearly increments without many efforts. This small firm is struggling to survive and will need tremendous effort to stand on its own legs. He thought they are only dreamers, selling hopes and assurance to pursue him.

Then a voice inside him said, "They are ambitious people and have determination to succeed."

Thirty persons attended this interview, only John was selected, as the first Indian drawing office staff member of L&T by the three founding members.

In his early twenties, he immediately recognized the growth potential of this small firm which was still struggling to survive. He trusted their words and had faith in these three great men's ability to transform the engineering landscape of India.

At that time L&T was without a project in hand, it was not having a drawing room, or design setup, so John was able to convince them that since it does not have this setup, he would-be part-time worker, and will do all their drafting work at naval dock, they agreed. So, he did not resign from the port trust but continued to work for both.

During the Second World War, the sea near dock is over crowded with warships and merchant ships, that needed servicing and repairs. L&T observed and there is had great potential in it, but it did not have expertise in it, fortunately it had at hand William Benedictson a person with experience in mechanical works. Also, John has completed his ship repairing course from Royal Navy, experienced in repairing Naval wars ships.

After hearing about John back ground, experience in naval ship repairs, L&T was convinced, it has the right man at hand, that's what they were looking for, at the time of world war, rare to find such a person. L&T was always far ahead in thinking, dreaming and confident about the future, when it had one table space only, and no space for drawing room or another person to seat in this room at the same time, it put an advertisement for a draftsman.

After some days, John received another hand written letter at home confirming his selection. At first John hesitated to join these three engineers, who were just offering ideas to please others. Even when some clients visited them, to meet and discuss a proposal, it was one person at a time. Two persons were seated inside and two stood outside.

Before 1942 L&T had already supplied some imported dairy products and machinery to the British army in India, to fulfill this demand it depended on imports. L&T did not expect the war will continue and extent to many countries, and the imports would stop due to war, when imports stopped, they were in a fix, unable to fulfill the orders in hand for dairy machinery and products. Import substitutes,

Delays and uncertainty continued, it tested their

patience, whether to stop this business and tell the British we cannot help it. Next what is the alternate left, shall we manufacture the same dairy machinery locally?

 L&T's team of three engineers, believed same Danish dairy machinery imported before, we can conceive and manufacture same here, after referring old catalogs and manuals of machinery and some supplied to British army already existing with us. L&T's warehouse at Calicut Street, Fort Bombay, was without a drawing room, toolroom and fabrication shop.

Only thing that the founding team of four men possessed was a will and determination to move forward with what had been imagined, to practical implement their dream of manufacturing it here. "We can measure the specifications of existing machines remaining here, draft new plan to manufacture it. When the two dreamers wanted to convert their dream into reality, the other two members of this founding team did not hesitate to support them, they encouraged them and all said" yes" it is possible," that was rare team spirit, and extraordinary character attitude, they all possessed to move this small firm forward.

As per orders, they visualized one machine at a time, one drawing was drafted by John at naval dock secretly and modified by them many times, at last it was approved. John and Larsen frequented nearby fabrication workshops, to explain this drawing to the workers, John further simplified the explanation in the local language, since their English ascent and language was not properly understood by them. They took their turn corrected and guide the work men on what was actually needed. Most of the work was segregated and material was out sourced locally by them, work was done at local workshops as per their direction. This was L&T's first manufacturing experience, when it started to manufacture dairy machineries locally. Quality control and pre delivery inspection was mostly first done by Larsen and John, later on Toubro and Benedictson came in and gave their approval. These dairy machines supplied to the Army and Navy stores worked well. This initial success, gave L&T the confidence, and the daring required for further adventure into the new and unknown fields of engineering.

The world is at war, there is heavy fighting in Europe and Fareast, at most other parts of the world, except in Bombay.

Daily newspapers printed horrible inhuman pictures of killings, torture and destruction of cities. The casualties of war were mounting and wide spread everywhere, that medical facilities or hospitals at conflict sites were insufficient or unable to bear this burden. After reading the printed newspapers and hearing radio news, the atmosphere in India is full fear and suspicion, people think this world will end soon, trust deficit is wide spread, that businessmen had stopped thinking of new business.

For lack of new business, negative thoughts filled the founders' minds and there was fear that we will have to close this firm at any time. Then only option left for us (Danes) is to return back to Denmark and join the war and get killed. They did not desire go back, due to war, other alternative left for Danish men was to remain here and succeeded. They decided, it is better to struggle and to stay safe here.

With all these efforts L&T's cash flow was inadequate, business orders were irregular and profit margin was poor. They thought we cannot survive without more business, it is war time and no new business is coming, how can we can support ourselves and some workers? If we needed to continue, we need to make more profits? Time is such a man good qualification and experience has no value, whether he is an engineer with ideas, or a common uneducated man, on the warring fronts all were equal, dressed in same uniform.

From these past mistakes L&T realized, there is no demand for their past skills and we must accept the fact that our experience is not suitable during the war. Our efforts are not bearing fruits. L&T must change and adjust according to market's demand; if not, it will close down. Alternate was to find a business that had scope during the war.

During their evening walks along the coast line, they observed the sea is always over crowded with ships, they found the answer and declared that the solution lied in finding business of ship repairs.

Chapter no 5

A strong nation

To become strong and prosperous nation, Japan did not possess enough coal and iron for steel industry, it is also a hilly country, short of farmlands for food and minerals for basic industries.

 To solve these problems, in1931 it attacked Manchuria and captured it. By 1937/38 most part of eastern China was under Japanese control, thus it was able to fulfill its industrial needs.

Japan imported eighty per cent of oil from USA and realized without oil it was at the mercy of Western powers which controlled most of it and they even control south East Asia rich in minerals like oil, rubber, rice etc.

"Japan is like a fish in a pond which water is being gradually drained away" A top naval officer told Emperor Hirohito.

1941 General Tojo took over as Prime minister of Japan, he believed, use of force is the best way to solve disagreements.

1940 most of Europe was under Hitler's control General Tojo imitated him and followed his example of surprise attack without warning, 1941 Japan attacked American naval base at Pearl Harbor in Pacific, damaged eight war ships, destroyed hundreds of aircrafts, killed 2000 men. USA joined the Second World War.

Japan was expanding fast inside and outside China, it captured Vietnam, Malaysia and was inside Burma, a British territory. Then Indonesia on 25th December 1941 it captured Hong Kong, two months later Singapore. By 1942 it captured whole of Philippines, only to be defeated at Midway Island. The fear of Japanese attack prevailed in India.

Turning point

By1942, Britain the workshop of the world was isolated by the German U boats, aircrafts pounded London. The German navy ships were in the Atlantic and the sinking of British ships had reached crises proportion that essential supplies for public plus raw material from outside for its industries were erratic. " For self-defense, all merchant ships must be demagnetized and fitted with guns. "The British Admiralty declared.

By end of 1942, the British Admiralty had instructed Bombay port trust to prepare an estimate for a detail tender to be published in the newspapers.

The offering was to manage first emergency floating dock in Bombay harbor called M.V. Hilda by British Admiralty, work consist of ship repairs, conversion and arming, fitting guns on merchant ships, machine guns nets, conversion and bridge protection, degaussing equipment designed to demagnetize and protect them from magnetic mines.

At end of the tunnel L&T saw light and had to face competition from some reputed firms for this tender. L&T had confidence it could manage show with experience in mechanical aspects of cement plants and John in ship repairs.

Before publishing this tender, the Royal naval command had already involved HMI naval yard in preparation of its cost estimate, so John was aware of labor and material prices quoted for it, for he was aware of the costing done for many ships. On the opposite side, when L&T was preparing the quotation (tender costing), he was also feeding them with the necessary inputs. L&T was happy that it had advance intimation about the tender costing and was able to quote reasonable rates. John being optimistic, did it voluntary without any monetary consideration in mind as he wanted this new company to survive, so he helped it.

After some negotiations luck favored L&T, it got the job and received advance money. It purchased the floating dock called M.V. Hilda to complete the given job.

Back to the pavilion

Before1943, L&T was sick a child, cash flow was bad and survival was difficult. Now with this work and cash in hand, it was over joy and confident that future looks better. Another important point was the work in progress was connected and carried on at HMI naval dock, where John worked, the man in control of the workshop is our coworker John, who is supervising two jobs at same time and with one bullet killing two birds. He is attending two jobs first to repair Royal navy war ships and then he also attending L&T's work, concerning the demagnetizing and fitting of the guns to merchant ships.

L&T did not object to John double role, the war was in need of his ship repairs experience and in turn L&T also needed his advice. They utilized his drafting skills for drawings and his experience in fitting guns on the ships to make them defend themselves.

The naval dockyard had a modern tool room with

many kinds of machinery; turning, milling, grinding and welding tools, fabrication and finishing workshops also, many types of jobs were carried on here. John was also trained here and L&T was permitted to utilize these facilities for the work in progress. William, Larsen and Toubro frequented these workshops, to supervise the machining and other jobs. In between John observed Larsen presence here, he was lost in his own thoughts, as how to realize his dream without these workshops? It is here many new ideas came to his mind and he desired a similar set up, to make his dream come true. Standing here he visualized tomorrow that one day he would build a factory with design room, drawing room, toolroom and fabrication workshop. This current assignment in hand, it built L&T's confidence and improved their perceptions, developed a strong desire to move forward beyond this work. Sometimes Larsen perceptions turned into his own hallucination experiences, that L&T is already a big company with complete factory setup. While doing this job L&T believed and realized the future is sunnier.

John had helped L&T to win this naval contract, but both were inexperience in execution and management these type projects. William Bendictson was the veteran with experience in different variety of projects in England. He was the Chief engineer in charge of this project, later when foundation of ECC laid, he was made the chief engineer of ECC at the foundation ceremony in 1944 at Mallet Bunder. As the execution moved well and billing continued, it made good profits. Both engineer and draftsman had injected new blood into this leukemic child's veins and made him fit to walk. Born again L&T was happy to get a new lease of life.

Chapter no 6

Bombay dock inferno

L&T's main operation theater was the Bombay dock, where the work in progress was still going on (to demagnetize ships and fit them with guns).

Like innocent children, L&T's founding team of four men frequented this place daily, to complete the work in progress. It was peak period of war and the dock was over crowded with ships, men and material, all movements were on war footing.

On 12 April 1944 freighter SS Fort Stikine arrived at Bombay from Karachi, carrying a load of mixed cargo, of cotton bales, 31 crates of gold bars worth £890,000, each bar weighted 25kgs, 1,400 tons of sensitive "A" types explosives like torpedoes, mines, shells plus barrels of oil and timber.

 Berthed in the Victoria Dock without raising a red flag, to indicate, it had sensitive cargo, about which ship's captain A J Naismith had protested before loading it at Karachi.

After two days of waiting for a berth at the dock, for unloading this cargo, at 14:00 afternoon on 14 April 1944, the ship crew noticed a fire onboard and pumped large quantity of water into the ship but they were unable to extinguish it. The thick smoke, prevented them from finding the source of fire.

At 15:50 afternoon, the order to abandon ship came, it was followed by a great explosion, with a terrific thundering sound that filled the air, and scattering debris in all directions. Which ignited more ships berthed close by? As this inferno started and now gathered strength, more and more devastating blasts occurred every now and then, from other ships parked nearby, with bum bating volcanic sounds waves continuously reversing from here and there.

As per record, the sound of these explosions was heard as far as 80 km away, even the sensors placed in Shimla, Himachal Pradesh far north of India recorded them.

But the people working in the Bombay dock and in the city were blind to the cause of this fire? They were abruptly terrified and shocked, Wondered, if a volcano had just erupted inside the dock and was emptying its stomach, full of hot lava in all directions.

Most people were frightened and some visualized it to be a Japanese attack, others an act of god that wanted to take revenge for their sins. There was commotion inside the dock, near the gates; on the roads, in the local transport, panic had griped them and were seen running in all directions, to saves their lives.

This warship had blown off, many ships parked close to it, nine ships were seen sinking and the burning debris from this explosion flying many miles away. This dock fire had set ablaze the surrounding Fort area, important developed business district of Bombay and ruin it. The debris from the ships, some flew and landed on houses close to Colaba area in the south, and others followed north direction, Sandhurst road and Dockyard railway stations.

GOLD BRICKS BECOME ROCKETS.

Since this ship was also carrying 31 crates of gold bars, weighted 25 kgs each, the pressure of this explosion was huge, it turned the gold bars into rockets, taking to the sky and then reversed, and landed here and there, some inside persons room, lucky to escape without injury, to receive gold bricks as god gifts. There are many stories related by old residents of this city, about these gold bricks, suddenly landing inside their residences, lucky ones later named their residences as god gifts.

Bombay dock fire killed more than two hundred people which included seventy-one firemen and dock workers.

The business district called Fort, close to the dock, offices and houses were burnt down, people lost not only their livelihood but also their personal belongings, many were left with just the clothes on their backs.

It was estimated that about 6,000 firms were affected and 50,000 people lost their jobs.

L&T lost its office at Nicole street Ballard estate and workshop at Calicut street, Fort area, fire had consumed all its records and goods.

Firefighters worked day and night and it took three days to bring the fire under control. 8,000 men toiled for seven months to remove around 500,000 tons of debris and bring the docks back into action.

The government took full responsibility for the disaster and monetary compensation was paid to the companies and citizens.

During the war news was censored, hence people were not aware, what the real cause of this dock fire was?

Two days later Japan Saigon Radio gave the correct news, a very strong explosion had occurred inside a ship parked inside the Bombay dock.

 This disaster occurred in the afternoon, in the presence of L&T founding team, consisting of four men William Bendictson, H.H. Larsen, S.K.Toubro and John A Gonsalves, when they were busy, engaged in executing their contracted work in the dock. They were shocked but brave not to panic, to face this misfortune head on. They did not to give up but struggled, to find way out of the dock and to escape. At the cost of their lives, all four somehow managed to escape, unhurt from this burning inferno, on the road to dance and embrace each other.

God saved L &T's inception team, for He had better plan in His mind for them and for India.

They saw hundreds of people running in panic state, trying to escape from the dock. Some fighting this blaze, others trying to save people trapped inside the dock, many getting trapped, some being roasted alive. Hundreds lost their lives.

(Bombay dock fire memorial, with a plate found in
the remaining ashes.)

 They remained as eyewitnesses to this greatest
explosion in the history of Bombay dock, called "the
Bombay dock fire," to recollect and relate this
horrible incident to others, an unfortunate
experience of life.

In honor of this event, two memorials were built one
at Ballard estate and another at Byculla fire brigade
station in Bombay which consisted of a pillar
attached with the plate, found in the remains of the
Bombay dock fire depicting this event.

When this small company just started to walk on
firm ground, after years struggle and it showed some
profits, an unpredictable event happened, which

gave them a lesson, in projects executions never give up, faced it head on, whatever comes and find solutions, finally triumph. This initial experience had great impact on the minds of founding team of four men.

This experience became principle of management for L&T, laid strong foundation of training, in executions of import substitutions and projects, "NEVER TO GIVE UP, BUT TO HAVE FAITH, PATIENCE AND HOLD ON STILLTHE FINISH."

This event inspired L&T in 1957 to acquire second head office building, the near the dock, for recollections of their lives spent in Bombay dock, remained with them, it also followed them like a ghost.

.

Chapter no 7

Birth of a firm called

Engineering Construction Corporation.

L&T started at Calicut street, fort area, with one small room that had space for one table only, it converted old this office into a storage place cum workshop.1941 it rented another office space at Nicol street, Ballard estate Bombay, which also consisted of one table space only. There was no place for drawing room, hence all drafting work of L&T was done at the Naval dock by John.

1944 Bombay dock fire had burnt down both these places, located near the dock, at the Fort area and Ballard estate in Bombay, office records went up in flames and then turned into black ash. That it affected firm's working environment, "HNS naval dock is still there in same place, where is L&T? and its name plate?"' John wondered,

some days after the explosion, he went in search of it. From these ashes, it put claim and got compensation from British government, a good sum, it gave them new hope.

Now with money in hand, L&T wanted everything to be at one place, (i.e office, drawing office, stores plus workshop). It purchased a large warehouse cum office shed from the Bombay port trust at Mallet Bunder, (Ferry wharf) now called Bhawhocha Daka in Dockyard, Bombay. It is one story iron I channel shed, ground floor plus one, office cum drawing room on the ground floor, first floor was used to store machines spares, tools etc, equipment was store in another shed behind this shed, which was also used as repair workshop.

 This shed is situated opposite to the dock area of large wooden dhows that once sailed the Arabian sea to Africa and Gulf countries, transport goods to and from to Bombay. From ECC office, you can watch the freight being loaded and unload here, from these wooden dhows. There is also a fishing dock located close by, boats daily docked and unloaded their large catch here, then it is transported from here to other places for sale. L&T's founding team found of fish, enjoyed dishes prepared from this fresh fish catch for lunch.

Two Danish men were ambitious and serious to make this small firm stand on its own legs and grow soon; John was always optimistic, had helped them to achieve their dreams, now it was on solid ground able to compete with other companies. L&T treated him as a friend, so he was contained to work with them. He also loved new and exciting work, always something new was placed on his table, to experiment and learn from it, monthly salary was paid on time.

Initially both partners had the determination to succeed, so they shared their original thoughts or ideas first among themselves,

Those days L&T freely shared their ideas with William and John, and then they discussed it thoroughly between team of four men before implementing it.

 Wanting to set up a new firm called Engineering Construction Corporation, they spoke to about it to William and John, sort their opinion and support, who suggested that engineering and construction business requires proper planning, designing, material procurement and execution, it also requires different types of technical skills personnel like engineers and experienced manpower in civil mechanical electric work. It should remain separate from other businesses, to take up more challenges in different fields of engineering, designing, fabrication and construction, L&T agreed.

Now L&T realized that sharing of their thoughts and accepting other people's good suggestion is a better style of functioning. When L&T grew and became a big organization, it continued same tradition. In 1964 a suggestion scheme was arranged at Powai, it provided the workers a way of communication with the management i.e. staff and employee were given chance to express their thoughts and share ideas in improving efficiency, reduce cost of manufacture, suggest alternative material, import substitution etc. Employees were told to express ideas in writing and submit the same to selection team. They were happy to know their views are also considered, their suggestions in writing were accepted, the employee was rewarded best suggestion.

A separate company called "Engineering Construction Cooperation" (ECC) was established in 1944 at Mallet Bunder.

L&T had great regards and respect for William Bendictson, a veteran civil engineer with many years of experience in executing civil, mechanical, electrical projects in U.K. and Europe. As both partners had less experience in construction projects, he was regarded the founder, made the first chief engineer in charge of ECC, who laid the foundation of this esteem company.

 At its inauguration, a group photograph was taken and it showed William Bendictson seated in the center with Larsen and Toubro on the either side of him. John is standing in second row behind them. The first team of ECC consisted of just fifteen people, these four men plus some workers, one copy of this photograph was framed and hung on the wall of John's house.

Mallet Bunder is still retained by L&T, as a nostalgia place and the birth place of its sister concern, Engineering Construction Corporation LTD, (ECC). It was L&T's first head office, showing the humble beginning, it was from here, they gradually realized their dream, it was slowly getting materialized and was coming true.

After successful execution of the port trust job, L&T gained confidence; it could venture into new fields of engineering where it had little or no experience at all, (naval dock job was in different field) for they always believed in doing new things and thus gaining experience and knowledge from it.

"We try to do difficult things, we don't shirk away

from intricate new tasks, and also we are quite prepared to give things up, so quite often when we have developed a line and it becomes easy, too easy, we give it up to "the bazaar" i.e. smaller industries which are rapidly coming up in India." Larsen commented.

With a small team of dedicated and discipline people, ECC was ready like a sportsman to face any competition in the field of civil, mechanical and electrical jobs. It quoted for small Railway tenders and got the small jobs, which kept L&T alive. The team faced the challenge in getting new jobs and also in completion of the job in hand within given time. But they never loss hope and perseverance to move on. Staff and workers showed their ability to perform the given work, as per the clock which these to two partners insisted on.

This same Mallet bunder shed was used by ECC for than fifty years.

Working style, Larsen and Toubro both were hard working, more particular about maintaining the office timings. L&T stood at the gate and saw their staff and workers reported to duty on time. When the work was on, they were more demanding to complete given job within the specified time. They did not believe in wasting time and were present at the site, open to discussion to solve the problem soon.

 L&T believed in hard work and discipline was the road to success. John understood what L&T expected of him and their style of working. So, he had already groomed himself and knew how to survive with the founders of the company.

Only real jewel in Larsen's crown was "Time." "Look at the watch John, time is limited." He often commented. Larsen believed and knew every person survived for limited period of time; it must be utilized carefully. To install discipline in his workers, he stood at the gate to observe and saw that the staff and workers reported to work in time. The initial L&T team had tough time to maintain the tempo of the work with the precision as per Larsen expectations. But L&T understood the worker's limit; John and L&T were all-rounder's, involved with every aspect of the work during company's childhood.

To complete the job within given time or ahead of it, L&T not only insisted workers first reported for duty in time but also insisted on given time to complete the job in hand, they visited the site, to know the real problem faced by the employees. Then they supervised and guided the staff and workers how to finish the given job in time. Whenever L&T made an appointment, they always expected the man to keep his word and reach in time.

John believed in same philosophy and followed it religiously hence they liked him and became good friends. But when the job was completed, there was also time for celebration.

By now Toubro knew John's character and trusted him, they became close friends, whenever they had free time, he loved to talk, crack jokes, sometimes he poured out his inner thoughts. He found there was none better friend than John to joke and talk. Both(L&T) were most seen spending their tea breaks with John together and exchange their personal experiences of life and work. Outside the office, there was no question of boss or worker, Larsen, Toubro and John were just friends, they liked to joke, or relate a tale of humor.

Toubro first desired to understand the project in hand better, hence he sorts more job details, once the whole idea was in his head, he became serious to finish it soon.

Larsen had leadership qualities, the drive and the

determination to implement ideas and turn it into reality. They were serious to a complete given task in time and remained in the office till late in the night and got it done. They collaborated with other companies, and acquired know, how to manufactures new products.

Their long childhood friendship was based on trust and individuality, to supervise and independently execute the given work and take responsibility for the work done. L&T offered better pay, even celebrated with the staff to make them feel they belong to a family. L&T made workers feel that they care for their welfare, in return staff and workers felt good and continued to work with the same company for long years.

Chapter no 8

1945 End of Second World War

It was greatest war fought on earth, it was wide spread in Europe, the Atlantic and Pacific Oceans, far east, Burma.

 After many years of fighting, killings, suffering, pain, loss of loved ones and homes, destruction of many famous cities like Berlin, London had happened in Europe.

The world over, people had witness it all, many events of mercy less killings, wretchedness, miserable destruction of cities and horrible living. They were fed up, they thought, this war was all full of madness, they long for peace, daily they prayed for it, eagerly waited for a new dawn to come, when serenity would prevail over the insanity.

L&T were exile for seven years and could not visit their native place, always hoped and longed for world war to end one day, then they will return to Denmark and see their parents, relatives and friends. They had also visualized a better tomorrow after the war, with peace there would be prosperity.

 The end came, when Russians troops reached Berlin by April1945 and the war drama on the western side was over.

On the pacific side, Japan did not give up. Albert Einstein had helped USA to manufacture atomic bomb. The real end to the Second World War came, when USA dropped first atomic bomb on Hiroshima on 6th August and second on Nagasaki on 8 August 1945, these atomic bombs had completely wrecked human habitat of two cities Hiroshima and Nagasaki in Japan, beyond recognition, they were crushed to ground beyond recognition, its previous existing infrastructure became a skeleton. The radiation effects of atomic energy on humans and animals were horrible and inhuman, the skin peeling off from human and animals' bodies. First time in the history of human race, all types of living creatures of Japan, who had experienced the horrors of nuclear bombing, looked like aliens on earth.

Japan surrendered to the U.S.A. in September 1945.

"The Second World War has ended," radio declared this big news and it continued to repeat it many times, in order to convince people, the world war has actually ended. In the morning this news was put it in print, by daily newspapers, still people did not believe this war has ended and Peace is present, it was difficult to make them understand.

With this news, a new dawn appeared on the horizon, like rays of sun actually contained gold dust and was spraying it on the ground, observing it, mood changed everywhere, smiling faces jumped with joy, to breath in new fresh air. The blue planet felt the calm and people felt relieved, from acts of war.

A long period of mourning, roads were filled with shining and laughing faces, People are Free from fear, extremely happy, free to move without fear of killing and destruction. Not born free but could roam free, peace gave them, hope of better tomorrow and time to celebrate.

People were dancing on the streets, smiling, cracking jokes, celebrating in restaurants and homes, everywhere there was joy, to mark the end of the greatest war on earth.

During the war, the British had imposed travel ban, travelling to Denmark and Germany was prohibited. So, L&T could not return to their native place, they were exiled for more than seven years here and William for four years here, many other Danes were imprisoned, also could not return home. When they heard radio news that world war has ended, it was thrilling and full of excitement, they had waited long for it, they were home sick and impatient to see their native land and their loved ones.

Mallet Bunder L&T's head office cum store, on hearing news that the war has ended, the mood at work had changed all were extremely happy, the Danes danced and embraced each other inside the cabinet. Suddenly John heard some loud voices, saw movements inside the cabin, through the glass partition, he also noticed the excitement that the work had stopped and they were happy smiling. They signalled him inside to convey this exciting news that the world war had ended. Also, Denmark which was under Nazi control was liberated by the British.

The disposition of three men had changed, now their talks were about freedom and celebration, of returning home to native Denmark, to see parents, relatives whom they had missed to see for past seven to eight years.

They had waited for "The longest day," to come, to be free from exile and return home.

In the evening L&T celebrated this event with William and John in a restaurant. Another photo of John celebrating with them in a restaurant was also in the house. It was an emotional get together for the persons in exile, who got very excited, started to express and pour out their feelings, which they had suppressed for a long time, how their decision to take refuge in Bombay was right, for it was the safest place in the world, to be and make a new beginning. There was fighting everywhere, especially in Europe and the far east if they had been there, they would not be alive today.

Three persons were in excitement, in a mood never seen before.

"Being safe and not joining the Nazis was correct, if we had joined them, we would be dead by now." Larsen opened himself up.

'" Bombay was the right place to be during the war, there was fear but also calm.""

"We could move about; we went on with our business, thank you god and Bombay, for keeping us safe and busy. " He added.

"Yes, decision to stay back was right." Toubro added.

"Being in exile and making a new beginning, we were engaged in created work, concerned with our knowledge. It was a humble beginning, with no financial help from outside, we began small, with only hope left with us, one day we will be successful. We enjoyed our working at Nicol street with one table space, the place was very small, and it did not fit us all at same time in the room. That's the humbleness and patience required for start-up." William commented.

"We had the determination to continue for four years, even when business was not coming, the fighting spirit, not to give up, have faith, we will be succeeded, we did it." Larsen added.

There was silent for a while.

"There was no alternate left but to stay here and struggle."" Toubro said.

"Now I want thank you all, for your wonderful company I had in exile, hard work that kept us busy and made us forget the realities of war, home, parents and relatives in Europe." William continued.

"I have decided long back when war ends, to return to Europe and devoted my time towards reconstruction of ruined places. God so desired and kept us safe here, I thank God and thank you all for the wonderful company, and unity of purpose to succeed."

He ended his speech and shakes hands with them.

"Stay back, the freedom struggle is strong and British rule in India will come to an end, within one or two years, when India is free, we will have tremendous opportunities." Larsen advised him.

"That's right, it's becoming very difficult, for them to hold on," Toubro supported him.

"I came here for temporary stay and when the war ends, then to return to my home." He replied.

"London and Europe ruined and they are in need of my project experience, there are also opportunities there." He added.

"We had the same thought, but we see better opportunities in India." Larsen advised.

"It's your dream and I wish to be here, but my mind is on the other side. God's blessing be with you all." William ended the speech.

German cities were flattened by Allied bombing and basic infrastructure was damaged in many places in Europe, cities infrastructure, houses were ruined, and millions were homeless. There were dead bodies of humans and animals lying on the streets, there were shortages of food and essential items, people were starving, surviving on whatever, they got to eat; even the flesh of dead animals was not left.

After the war William Bendictson returned to England and devoted his time to rebuild this ruined place. Larsen went back to Denmark and then visited many European firms and discussed collaboration with them. He came back with new ideas and advice Toubro follow it up, when he is in Denmark.

During the war, some Danish men were caught for supporting the Nazis and imprisoned in Bombay, now after the war they were released from the Indian prisons, ECC accommodated them, they worked with it for some time, then left for Denmark.

In October 1945 L&T told John, you must resign from Bombay port trust and work with us full time. L&T had secured small contracts from railways and it still wanted more business; it was struggling to stand on his own legs. John resigned his job and devoted full time for the company. Those days all three remaining team members were all-rounders, engaged in many types of activities, what this company needed to keep it moving and make it survive.

Larsen had also visited other places in Europe, and he was able to convince European companies, to collaborate with L&T, to share new ideas, modern techniques, sign collaborations, or he was willing to purchase licenses and design specifications from them, to manufacture new items in India.

Next Toubro went on leave to Denmark and was instructed to do the follow up, Larsen waited for his return, with signals of willingness from European companies to collaborate, when both were in Bombay, they discuss new ventures and financial aspect of it.

L&T had a burning desire to set up new engineering cum manufacturing unit in Bombay, but it lacked finance, so it frequented the Danish consulate, some friends and industrialists with its ideas; to get financial help to establish a new company here. It was able to convince them and got financial help. After the world war, L&T partnership was dissolved as one partner William Bendictson had left it.

On 7 the February 1946 L&T partnership was converted into L&T PVT LTD, here at Mallet Bunder, to raise additional capital required for more adventures, of building a new factory for manufacturing different items or for signing new collaborations with foreign companies.

Chapter no 9

Mallet Bunder

A nostalgia place called Mallet Bunder, old head office of ECC and L&T, old timers who had worked here, visit this place sometimes and recollections of good old days spent here are mirrored in front of them.

After the war, a new dawn appeared at Mallet Bunder, the rays of sun glittered like real gold is mixed in it. Without the sound of the gun fire and smoke, peace had given L&T the new hope of a better future that lied ahead.

This office at Mallet Bunder is situated close to the dock, in front we can see the large wooden dhows, unloading and loading of cargo, brought from Gujarat and other far-off places like Africa.

Larsen's dream

The 1944 Bombay dock fire had caused great damages to many parts of Bombay dock and also to Fort business areas. The Royal naval dock had full set up for repairs of Navy ships, tool room, fabrication, finishing workshop, it was full with all types of imported machinery, plus others finishing items. These machines and tools were utilized for ship repairs, it was still in good working condition. John was trained here in these workshops about ship repairs. L&T had a small office set up in the naval dock, when the work in progress was on i.e. degreasing and fitting guns on the merchant ships to make them fit to defend themselves, Larsen frequented the tool room and was often found hallucinating inside it, thinking how he would acquire, this type of whole setup, especially machinery for his dream factory. He always had a desire and fantasized off buying it.

In 1946 Bombay port trust put an advertisement in newspapers for sale of many damaged items as it is, the naval dock tool room items, and many things were also put for sale.

Now after inspection L&T found it worth, so it quoted for this tender, and purchased many machineries. It transported and kept it at Mallet Bunder.

Thinking when L&T's new factory shed is ready at a new place, it would transport the same machinery from Mallet Bunder to the factory.

Engineering Construction Corporation (ECC) at Mallet Bunder, Dockyard, Bombay was a new born child, it quoted for the Railways work tenders, and managed to secure small jobs. The work in progress was on; small team kept hope of a better tomorrow, and also visited the sites to see the work completed.

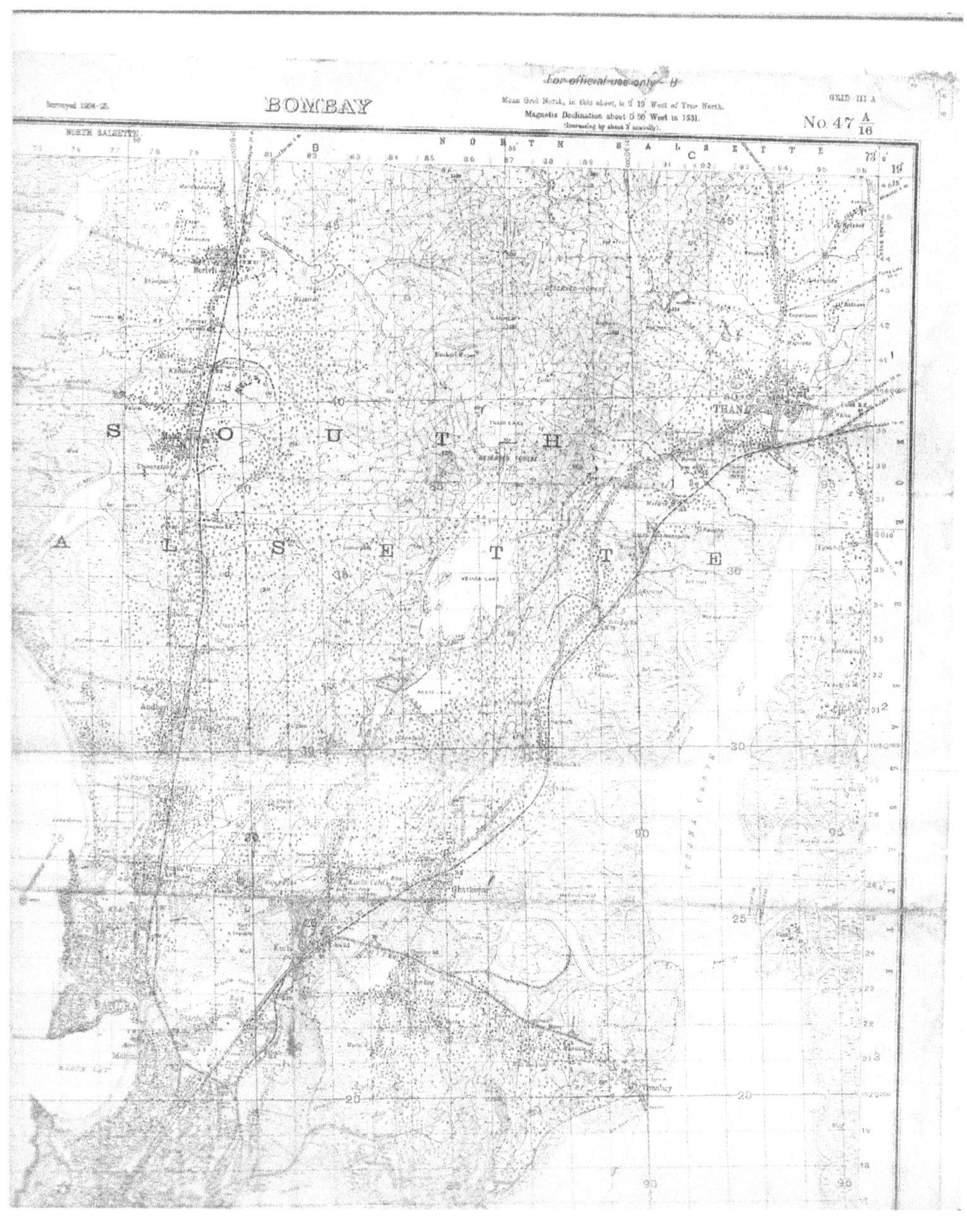

Refer map on this page

(Larsen made a pencil sketch, he marked area

opposite Powai lake to be acquired by L&T)

This map of Bombay based on survey done in 1930

was used by the founding team of three men, to find a place, for L&T's first factory to be constructed. (This1930 map of Bombay is still there with John and kept in his bookshelf.)

1946 One day John is busy drafting, unaware Larsen had secured funding from business men, Danish consulate and others to establish a new factory.

Larsen called John inside the cabin and unfolded the same map of Bombay on the table, based on the survey done before 1930, Toubro, John and Larsen surrounded the table and started to discuss where to locate L&T's first new factory.

This map showed city's boundary limits were within Main Island of Bombay (Mahim and Sion to Colaba in the south). In the north from Kurla to Thane and Bandra to Borivali, these areas consisted of thinly populated small villages, paddy fields, forest, mountains and mangroves salt pans. It also showed two railway lines and two roads that connected the main island to rest of Bombay state and whole of India.

"Where should we locate our factory?" Larsen

inquired and pointed his finger at different locations on the map

"Here or there. "He demanded.

Toubro and John could not guess which place was right by looking at the map, so they remained quiet. After this debate, three men visited some places in and around Bombay, discussed the advantages and drawbacks of various locations. Still Larsen was not satisfied, which was the right place? John wondered and then recollected his school picnics to Vihar and Powai lakes and the evergreen forest close by.

"Here sir, near the lakes with water. "John pointed his finger.

"We have not surveyed this place, let us first see it." Larsen demanded.

It was familiar location, Larsen and Toubro had also visited these lakes before, so they supported in John's opinion and agreed to survey the place.

Next day Larsen, Toubro and John visited Powai lake, (at that time, a long journey through the narrow unpaved road from Andheri to Powai), they stood in front of the gate of the Powai lake garden and surveyed the place in front, for ages it was thick evergreen forest, wild area without a passage through it. There was no human habitation close by.

They walked along this narrow road which went up to Vihar lake, then they returned to the same place where they first stood. As soon as they stared and pointed their hands at this forest, monkeys' gangs jumped down from the trees and came hauling at them, birds sounded alarms, all warned them to stay away from their native land. When they went towards the lake, they saw large crocodiles moving in and out of water, again they came back to the same gate.

They pointed their hands in front.

"Here this place is a suitable for our factory.

"Larsen said.

"To whom does this land belong to?"

"This forest land, we will inquire with collector's land records and find it." John replied

"If it is collector's land, we will not have much hindrance, also get a clear title." Larsen commented.

"Yes." John replied.

"Large forest land can be purchased in one deal." Larsen added.

"Right, Plus, we have the lakes to supply water close by." Toubro supported. "Tomorrow we will send someone to collector office and get the right information," he added.

Cool breeze, scenic lakes, evergreen forest, birds singing, monkeys swinging. This picnic was a fascinating experience, a memorable place that created a recollections and then hallucination experience of a wild paradise, if it is? it is here within this island.

After surveying the place opposite to Powai lake, L&T's founding team of three men returned to Mallet Bunder and agreed, it's correct place to build L&T first dream factory as visualized by them.

Next step, to purchase the land, they frequented the collector office, to get the license to establish a new factory, they were engaged with government offices.

Since India was still under the British rule, they followed free trade policy, the things were not so complicated, the officials were helpful, there was no land limits or ceiling, at one go they could purchase large tract of land, there were few restrictions or no bribes to be paid to get the license or clearances for the projects.

The government officials had a clear picture in their mind that this new company would generate employment and be good for all, hence did not delay but cooperated with founding team, thinking as per their look, they are all English men, perhaps with higher reach. They were able to complete formalities and get permission fast.

(Refer page 87 pencil making done by Larsen on the map showing land acquired by L&T.)

Now L&T had purchased large tract of forest land from the collector, covered with a thick blanket of evergreen forest. L&T got the property card from collector office with the map of the newly acquired land, place surrounding it. He placed it in front of John and directed him to first survey the place as per this map, then put marks on the trees as outside fencing on the area. Based on it to erect a fence around this acquired evergreen forest land.

This evergreen forest area in front of the Powai lake was the native land of wild creatures like the leopards, monkeys, foxes, snakes and crocodiles. These wild animals and birds had lived here for centuries, in harmony of their natural surroundings. Uninformed and dumb creatures were unaware of man intentions, to destroy their homes.

Now John was in charge of clearing this wet and murky forest land, infested with poisonous snakes and wild cats like leopards that remained in wait, hidden on tops of trees or nearby, ready to attack a human at any given opportunity. This forest also bird's paradise, the master piece of creation, filled with varieties of birds, unimagined or never seen before by wild life lovers like Larsen and him. Every morning singing a welcome melody, directed by conductor bird, created pleasant sounds like heavenly orchestra is just welcoming them.

John was fearless and courageous man, for whom L&T's words were like an order from a King to his authorized commander, once told to perform a task, he never looked back or protested, he only knew one thing, it must be obeyed and completed. He did not resist them or complained about the work, this is my duty and he took it as a challenge, thinking visualized dream by L&T must be fulfilled. He worked like a devotee to build this new temple of god, not only for L&T but also for India's industrial development. That was his spirit of devotion which helped L&T' to make fast progress. L&T' was fortunate to find a man of optimist character, who only though of the company's growth and ignored his incentives or cried for it.

At that time, there was no human habitation around Powai, hence for every basic need, hence he had to think and plan in advance, all the tools, food requirements, if he missed to carry one item less the laborers, they will get an excuse to stop work. From Andheri station he purchased the cutting tools like pickaxe shovels etc hired laborers, his team that would work under his instructions, then transported the men and material by horse carriages to Powai lake.

John frequented the area close to Andheri station daily, spent time with laborers, did necessary purchases, engaged horse driven carriages or bull carts that took half working hours in travelling to and from Powai, on through the thin and muddy road, as there was no regular bus service. Another drawback there was also no electricity or no telephone at this site.

Before John left Andheri Station, he had thought in advance of every possible need or equipment needed to commerce the work. For Powai was an isolated forest area, villages were situated far of at Marol and Kurla.

Initially for every small or big purchases, he depended on outdated mode of transport like bull carts or horse carriages. As lorry or jeeps did not agree to run on unpaved rough tracks or demand double return freight charges. Which L&T objected initially to save cost,

 Then he hired a lorry and brought some laborers with him to cut the evergreen forest and level the ground to erect fencing around this newly acquired land.

Before the axe fell on the trees, as soon as the workers approached the forest, group of monkeys jumped down and came forward to defend their land, resisted the takeover by pouncing on the workers. It was a daily, tug go war between the monkeys and workers with bamboo sticks, this drama went on for many days. When workers failed to drive the monkey gangs away, John got an idea and persuaded them with offerings of food, then some monkeys realized this man offered them fruits and became friends, trial and error method worked, little by little the area was cleared.

Food and fruits offering helped, sometimes entire basket was grabbed by monkeys, gradually they danced around him. Slowly the forest was cleared and the wood was daily loaded in the trucks and transported elsewhere, this work in progress took more than three months.

On the south side of Bombay Island, many Indians were fighting for India's freedom and shouted

"Freedom is my birth right", on the northern side, there were none to fight for the animals' birth rights, born free to live in their own land, where generations after generations had lived, as if they were aliens and had no rights to exist. God created the environment (land) for man only and not animals to be shared equally. The selfish man claimed its ownership and only thought about himself, only man had the rights to land, birds' animals rest were all aliens.

 Man's motive was to make profit and see the welfare of own kind. By clearing the forest and he acquired land to build factories. The animals and the birds were not of his kind, so they were excluded, they were helpless so they accepted their fate blindly, loss their land and freedom for man's progress. The city dwellers had given up cultivation and now only thought about employment, so they did not regret the loss of natural habitat, or about bad effects of industrialization. They did not visualize that decrease in forest cover would result in less oxygen supply to Bombay city, which in turn would increase the lung diseases like T.B. asthma etc. Soon L &T purchased own lorries, John daily carried his own Tiffin box with him, since there was no human habitation here, the question of a restaurant did not arise, or he will have to stay hungry.

During daily lunch time, some uninvited guests always stood close to him, apart from monkeys that sprang up, and snacked a piece, a friendly fox frequented and stood close by, he approached him at the right time for his share. All demanded their share, so he packed extra food to share his lunch with them also.

Even after the shed was built and had enough place for office inside, the founding team of three men, always preferred to keep their office outside in the open under the shade of a tree, without electricity, they felt it was more comfortable, cooling and refreshing outside than inside the shed. They also had their lunch in the open and shared it with dumb guest that frequented this place at the right moment. John had a copy of the property card in his hand, which showed the drawing of the acquired land, based on it he did the marking of the boundary as per collector's survey done before. Larsen or Toubro frequented this place and surveyed it again.

Those days the road from Andheri station to Powai was narrow and unpaved at many places. Without bus service, people travelled on horse carriages or bullock carts to these lakes. Even from Kurla, there was no bus service to Powai factory.

After clearing the forest and levelling the ground at Powai, same founding team of three men, (H.H. Larsen, chemical engineer S.K. Toubro civil engineer and John Gonsalves draftsman who had completed his course in repairs of Royal navy wars ships), planned and designed sheds and buildings based on European designs, elder sister concern ECC which then consist of a small team recruited more personnel and constructed them.

When sheds and building were completed, same tool machinery procured from port trust and utilized them during the war, was transported to Powai from Mallet Bunder. This fulfilled Larsen's dream of having same naval dock tool machinery for his new factory.

L&T had borrowed large amounts of other people money, so they were careful in utilizing it, initially it faced tough time to get business and to keep the cash flow moving. Up to1955 Best did not provide transport buses from Andheri or Kurla to Powai, L&T did not own any company buses hence did not provide free transport service to his employees on this route, it hired old private buses to transport the staff and workers to and from the Andheri to Powai. The roads were narrow and unpaved at many places, old buses moved slowly on and sometimes got damaged, they were not reliable, staff, workers found it difficult to reach the factory in time. Larsen got frustrated but could not help. He had to tolerate, since he did not have means to keep the tempo in time.

During the monsoon season, this narrow mud road was flooded which slowed movement of the buses, some buses with old rusted roof, the rain water leaked in through it, which compelled staff to open umbrellas inside it to protect themselves. The old workers and staff had the spirit of moving on, no grumbling or cursing the company, not to give up but to carry on whatever comes.

 L&T was still financially weak, it was living on borrowed money, since it had already borrowed from banks, friends, Danish consulate etc. Still, it wanted to raise more capital, partnership was converted into

Larsen &Toubro private ltd on 7th Feb 1946.

Luck opens another door.

After the world war in 1946, Caterpillar Tractor & co USA Company wanted to sell its large inventory of earth moving equipment, machinery, spares and move out of India, it was on lookout for an agent to represent its business interest in India, it put an advertisement in Bombay newspapers, L&T was convinced this is a golden opportunity, to venture into new business of heavy machinery, in sales, maintenance and repairs of heavy equipment, spares. It convinced Caterpillar Tractor Co. USA and showed them the Powai works the sheds being built for various activities, for sales of heavy earth moving equipment, spare parts, and servicing, it had the capability, thus it acquired this agency. An agreement was signed between them. This collaboration with Caterpillar was profitable and opened another door to make more profits. Later it helped the company to diversify in design, fabrication and manufacture of heavy machinery in India.

L&T got orders for designing and fabrication of milk storages tanks and bulk carrier tanks for transporting milk from one place to another. With ECC involved in engineering and construction, it quoted for new dairy projects which involved complete designing and fabrication dairy plant and equipment. When L&T got the job, both brother and sister collaborated in executing it.

After some years, more and more forest areas were cleared, around Powai and new companies occupied this land. But L&T was still a young child, struggling to make more profits to pay back the loans it had taken from different parties; things did not change soon.

It is only when L&T started to make good profits; the world eyes opened and people started to think and notice it progress. Before that it was a small unknown company. Larsen attributed L&T success to initial team of dedicated and capable men who put in great deal of hard work and stayed with company during the most difficult period of Second World War.

When factory at Powai was established, L&T approached European manufacturers of packaging machinery and collaborated with them, plant was set up to design and manufacture in India, produce tin products and cocks for bottling liquid, packs for biscuits, soaps etc.

L&T Powai

After the forest was cleared and more land was levelled, new factory sheds were designed on European designs by two founding fathers and drafted by John, ECC executed the civil mechanical and electrical works.

Now L&T had separate sheds for design room, tool room, fabrication and finishing workshops. Later it imported heavy machines and set up a well-equipped sheet fabrication plant

Chapter no 10

1947 L&T's first factory at Powai

Men with determination and courage, the fittest men survived the bad times of 2nd World War.

Great luck and randomness helped this L&T start up, when it had one table place for one person to seat, in the room and no drawing room to place the new draftsman, it put an advertisement for the vacancy of a draftsman. What luck John managed to do all their drafting work at naval dock.

During the Second World war, when fear and uncertainty gripped business community, even when businessmen saw opportunities, they were not interested in setting up any new companies. L&T started a partnership firm, as consultants, business was coming in their line of expertise. For the Royal navy's tender, of demagnetize and gun fitting on merchant ships, to make them defend themselves, when they were not experience in ship repairs, it quoted for Admiralty's tender to make merchants ships defend themselves, John had prepared the estimate for it, they were aware of rates in advance, it helped them to quote in competitively rates for the floating dock tender, by chance survived.

It was the first big contract secured by this firm, with high profit margin, it gave them confidence and hope they can live in India and win big contracts, can establish a company to manufacture products, bring in new European technology and develop new products, manufacture machinery and industrialize India and make big name.

Make in India

Between May 1938 and 15th August 1947, all four members of L&T's founding team had seen many strikes, born fires of English made textiles in Bombay, read about rebellions carried out by freedom fighters at different places in India, seen many leaders struggle for India's freedom _They remained silent witnesses to the freedom struggle. At the peak of this freedom movement against the English rule, they looked like Englishmen, the oppressor, they were doubted, as Englishmen and should be harmed. It was considered bad wear European clothes, suit with a tie, they were causal.

 The 1942 Quit India movement at August Kranti maidan Grant road Bombay, L&T lived close by and were able to see the crowds at this place gathered protesting British quit India.   L&T believed, when India is free and can frame its own policies, there would be tremendous opportunities in this virgin territory, for basic industries like steel, cements, dairy and in infrastructure. L&T would offer technical consultancy design the projects and execute them through the sister concern ECC, it would do the civil, mechanical, electrical work with or without technical collaboration, it took up challenges in dairy plant, machinery, railway works and infrastructure.

After Second World War, William Bendictson left L&T partnership, and returned to his native place England. Now the founding team consisted three members Larsen, Toubro and John, earlier, the same team had manufactured import substitutions here, without complete set up and outside help. They started to design the first modern factory at Powai based on European drawings and when work in progress was on, L&T quoted for new jobs and obtained some orders to manufacture dairy machinery and some works connected with railways. Now with some orders in hand, situation was different, L&T purchased technical drawings, specifications from aboard or collaborations with Danish firms, L&T built its own set up of infrastructure like design room, tool room, fabrication and finishing facilities. It recruited more people, since engineers were scare and difficult to find in India, they imported some Danish personals. As more persons were recruited, things were different, work was segregated and each department head was given certain responsibility, based on personnel skills, principle of division of labor followed. Initially the progress was gradual, based on trial-and-error methods used by them to manufacture and gain experience from it. L&T always believed in accepting new challenges and completing work, mostly with own experience. And it ventured into manufacturing of plant and machinery for dairy, cement, power, fertilizers, iron and steel.

Chapter 11

More at L&T's Powai

The fittest men survived the hard times.

Two engineers (the founders) designed L&T's first modern factory at Powai and when work in progress was on, it quoted for new jobs and was able to secure orders to fabricate dairy plants & products from local dairies like milk steel storage tanks, milk pasteurizers, milk bottlings plants, so on and more work force was added and the connection with manufacturing of dairy machinery continued.

Now situation was different L&T had built own design room, toolroom and other facilities, it had also obtained licenses, drawings and specifications from Danish dairy industry, so it was much easier to understand how to manufacture these machineries here.

L&T completed the orders in hand, as the development of dairy industry in India continued to grow, more orders were in hand. Still education was in its infancy and hence it was difficult to find engineers in India. It was the same team of three men, two engineers and one draftsman which relied on own experience, did all the thinking, debating, designing work. Inside the factory acted as supervisor or guide to the new children (staff and workers) thus they grew under better parents and in a good home and earned better income.

Mallet Bunder served as the head office of L&T. Again L&T approached some Indian businessmen and banks for help to establish a joint stock company and got funding. ~~L&T was not a well know e few people were aware of its humble beginning in Bombay that it was conceived by two technical educated Danish engineers, refugees trying to make good utilization of their time in ex~~When they were able to arrange these loans, it put in the application to Bombay stock exchange, for completing the formalities of registration with it, as a joint stock company, for its first initial public offering.

In the application to BSE same Danish name Larsen and Toubro limited was mentioned, so in the advertisement of initial public offering in Bombay newspapers, same name had to be put. So, the company's European name which sounded confusing to the Indian public remained, they wondered, whether it is Indian or European company? Inviting offers to invest in the shares of this newly registered joint stock company.

Many investors did not read the prospectus properly, the same Mallet Bunder Ferry wharf Dockyard Bombay, head office address of the company was mentioned. But Indian public, banks, institutions invested reading the scope of work it was engaged in, gave details of advance engineering and the future prospects of this diversified new engineering Co. For the public, it was difficult to believe, this Indian company possessed such skill and expertise in advance engineering like designing, manufacture and installations of dairy, cement, brewery plants, it could even engage itself in construction of big hydroelectric dams with the help of sister company ECC.

L&T also thought, should we change name? but they had already registered the company with BSE on the same partnership firm name, so they remained silent and watched the reaction.

Even though IPO mentioned brief history of L&T which was conceived and started in Bombay, first engaged in engineering consultancy, in designing of technologically advanced dairy/ cements plants, etc and also in execution civil mechanical and electrical works, it's a diversified new engineering Co, it has skills to execute basic projects like cement, dairy, brewery plants. Few people believed it is an Indian company had such capacity. It had mentioned its head office address is Mallet Bunder Ferry wharf in Bombay. The investors   note this, read brief notes of this IPO advertisement and understood it's potential, new free India needed such a company, for its progress and industrial development, it offers better future prospects.

After reading this advertisement, most investors contributed money thinking it is a European co. IPO was oversubscribed many times. After the success of this IPO, limited liability was added to the company name.

Fact that this company was started by two technically qualified Danish engineers, displaced by Second World War, was not known to the public.

Public was under impression that it is a European

company. First Initial public offering was over subscribing thinking it's an foreign company.

For L&T's first, initial public offer or IPO, the most money was contributed by Indian businessmen, Indian banks, institutions, rest by Indian public. So, majority of shareholders of L&T are Indians, except for L&T and few foreigners.

Gradually L&T started construction of more factory sheds at Powai in Bombay and recruited more and more Indians and they worked for it, people became aware, it is Indian company, with the factory located at Powai in Bombay.
Now the work was based on division of labour and segregated according to qualification and skill, experience, there were Danish experts imported to train personals. Now it was ready made joint stock company, thatThen, it provided work and livelihood to hundreds of -Indians, and most of staff and workers are Indians.

L&T always looked for challenges and thought of being different from others, since its initial stage to survive it took a different road, a murky road and less traveled on by others. To succeed the founding team always believed in hard work, in their own designs, fabrication or manufacturing facilities, Import substitutions, new machines or difficult things which were not made in India, were now made in India. From the beginning L&T's thinking was to engage its people in doing new things.

The situation had changed, in Bombay luck favored the refugees, not only to remained safe with families here, but also to venture into a new business of their interest and become owners of it.

 The English did not trust the Danes, they thought and feared these men would sabotage and damage the infrastructure or ports. During the war, Bombay was a safe place and far from the battle, hence they many Danes and other nationalities had taken refuge here, carried on here, as they found no alternative left but to be safe and live on, until the situation changes.

As years passed with new orders of stainless-steel milk storages tanks, milk pasture risers or to build complete dairy plants to store milk and produce milk products like curd, cheese etc. More work force was added to complete the orders in hand, so the connection with development of dairy industry in India remained and prospered.

Still, it was difficult, to find engineers in India, so the founding team mostly of two engineers and one draftsman, relied on own experience, did all the thinking, debating, designing work and even acted as supervisor and guide. Thus, founding team played the big role of parenting and schooling of new children, recruited for different works, they were trained and listened their advice. Thus, the childhood of staff and workers grew under the guidance of better parents and in a good home.

Mallet Bunder served as head office of both the companies, L&T's and ECC.

In India education was still in infant stage, schools were far, mostly in cities, level of literacy was low, technical colleges were few and only located in big cities. For the public, it was difficult to believe, this Indian company possessed such skill and expertise in advance engineering like designing, manufacture and installations of dairy, cement, brewery plants while at the same time engaged in design and construction of big technical advance projects.

People with engineering skill were rare, engineers were not available, L&T advertisements failed to get qualified engineers. Some Danish engineers were recruited and imported from Denmark to work here, and they also trained Indians in different skills that were needed.

 L&T since its initial stage to survive it took a different road, a murky road and less traveled on by other entrepreneurs. To succeed it believed in hard work and in doing difficult things, acting as consultants for setting up cement, dairy, breweries, packaging plants, from inception to finished plant, which were not manufactured here previously. It always looked for challenges and thought of being different from others, hence it did not venture into consumer products.

Now it had money to purchase technical knowhow or designs or also signed new collaboration agreements with Europeans companies to manufacture to manufactured bottle closures, other items imported from Denmark it started to manufactured heavy equipment previously imported here.

 Virgin place.

On15th AUGUST 1947 mother India was free, but her own body was now cut into two parts, India and

Pakistan. Like a mother, she felt pity and accepted large inflow of Hindu and Sikh refugees from Pakistan, the British army had vacated many military camps at various locations throughout India, so she accommodated them at these camps. In Bombay district, the British army had built many military camps along the coast line, now they had vacated them, at Versova, Bandra Worli, Chembur and other places like Kalyan and Uhlasnagar, refugees occupied these camps.

During the Second World War India sent manpower and material to fight this war and also had spent lot of money on it. Undivided India was rich country, still left with good balance of trade and surplus cash, with Imperial Bank in Bombay.

British had built the railways but the Indian peninsula was still not fully connected, being an agricultural economy, it lacked infrastructure and many basic industries like iron and steel, cement etc, it also needed schools, hospitals, there was severe food shortage and high inflation.

L&T as a public limited company quoted for these tenders and executed many civil mechanical electrical works, it was able to secure more orders and it built its own factories, offices on bank credit, it could plan and recruited many professionals as per orders in hand, with other people money it acquired huge assets like land and buildings. It became more diversified company.

Now as L&T made progress, provided better pay and good working facilities, free transportation in better class of buses. Herd followed and more people approached it for jobs and more managerial post filled. But the fact remained, would the present L&T employees would travel and work devotionally as John did in the past? It was his simplicity, humbleness and honesty plus his attitude to see others prosper, helped L&T to make tremendous progress.

Then came the so-called professionals, who brought in their induced knowledge to show their management skills, now accepted as progress and as latest techniques, they demanded more salary, comfort and job safety?

When professional came, they brought in division of labor and simplification of job, specialization, duty time was reduced, eight hours working hours per day, this encouraged workers to demand over time, which was considered bad before by the founders.

Whereas John did not think much about it, for L&T he was an all-rounder, obedient to them, so L&T as a startup, made him do many types of jobs which were needed, to stand and walk. He performed as their expectation, that's why L&T made progress tremendous progress within short period of time, from one table space only firm at fort to a company in Powai Andheri, Mumbai, that occupied the largest area, with many buildings and sheds spread everywhere within this area. As foretold by Larsen, during John first interview, he believed his statement, had faith in him that one day within L&T's structures there will be hundreds of tables will be laid for all. When this dream came true, tables were laid for professionals to seat and order others to do the same donkey's work. Now L& T was able to walk and stand on its legs, the profession thinking changed, they forgot about man who helped it to survive, cornered and left him in same posting while they got better ranks and medals.

To keep L&T 's technical engineering skills alive, they started a small firm, to keep them occupied and help them forget the past. During the war business environment was unstable and work was not coming, fear of Japanese attack filled the air. They kept hope and had patience, they pursued one goal after another as visualized by them, thinking they will try to survive here, till the Second World War ends and then return back home.

"Now great persons work with L&T, there was time, when it had one table and three persons, when one was seated inside, other two persons stood outside. Professional just peeped and left, would these persons believe Larsen's words that there will be hundreds of tables liad and join it then? Surely they would have ignored it." John commented.

"Forget job safety, even working for this company was very risky, during1944 Bombay dock fire, the inferno started in the afternoon, they were present in the dock, luck by chance the team survived and lived to build this company for others."

"But at that time, there were persons who had faith in L&T's ability to face challenges and overcome them, to quote for new tenders which demanded unknow engineering skills, which took time, first to understand the problem and then solve it. L&T had patience and determination to move on." John ended his comments.

Chapter 12

Small rat becomes a Fat elephant.

When L&T was an established company, the cash flow improved and profits increases, credit worthiness improves, more banks and institutions are willing to offer credit. It signed more collaborations or acquired design licenses either to manufacture new products and machinery or execute technically advance projects. It also acquired new companies, became diversified company, with many subsidiaries.

L&T GROUP consist of group of companies, specialized in different fields of engineering, manufacturing, fabrication, constructions.

1960 Utkal machinery was set up in technical collaboration Voith GHH and Koppers of Germany, plant was situated in rural forest area of Orissa state,1972 L&T drilling &equipment ltd in Madh Island Mumbai, L&T Mc Neil ltd at Chennai in technical collaboration of McNeil, Akron Ohio USA.

Eutectic Welding &Alloys of India Ltd, Tractors Engineers Ltd a joint venture between Caterpillar Tractors, Audio values
It purchased Hindustan Brown Boveri Ltd manufacturing special electrical equipment. **So,** on the list **of collaboration and acquisition** is unlimited, now it has gone into information technology or software development **and Finance or NBFC** etc.

To manage the whole show, it puts advertisements after advertisements, in search of engineers, and professionals that once ignored this firm, during its initial struggle. **More and more** new engineers **and professionals are** recruited as India is now full technical staff, other skill workers. **They are trained and still date, the company is managed well.**

Chapter no 13~~1~~

~~1912,~~ ____ – **Love at first sigh**

To spare the reader from boredom of repetition of same story of acquisitions or collaborations made by L&T. I have ~~Exciting~~added romance, Exciting **family history of John's wife** and how he meets her. Additional stories of L&T hobbies, awards **come** after this.

<u>1912,</u>

A large Caravan consisting of three Victorias (horse carriages) and three bullock carts loaded with men, rice bags; vegetables, clothes etc moved on the mud road from Kalina towards Bandra. Seated in the first open horse carriage was Anthony Dais, the Zamindar and his son Nicholas, were on an annual thanks giving trip to the Mount Mary church, where they would donate the luggage for the church and orphans taken care by the nuns.

The second carriage consisted of friends and third of the servants, the whole caravan moved on slowly, through the muddy rough roads, fields, ponds and open places. As the scenes of cultivated fields passed, it reached close to the Chuim village, in Khar, Nicholas is astonished after seeing a tall and fair girl, standing in the open field and busy plucking flowers. Fascinating by her personality, immediately all his attention moved towards her. He concentrated on her beauty and was capturing it his mind, he was loss in her thoughts, forgot his father Anthony seated near him and is observing him. Nicholas did not care who was watching him, he was more concerned about the girl than his father. Anthony understood his son feelings.

"He likes the girl and is off marriageable age." Anthony said to self.

Soon he ordered. "Stop the caravan."

He got down from his carriage and went to the gate of the farm and stood near it. Surprise to find a handicap man supported by a wooden stand stood close to door of his house. Anthony Dais knocked on the field gate, the man took two steps forward but his daughter Lizzy ran to open the gate. She unlocked the wooden gate and stood close to it. They both exchange glances and he admires her structure, he shoot the scene, a close up.

"I am Anthony Dais, the Zamindar of Kalina, would like to meet your father." Anthony introduced himself.

"Okay come in." She replied.

Dais moved close to the man but before he could open his mouth.

"Mr Dais, what made you stop your carriage here and approach me." Fernandez said recognized him.

"It is our common interest," Dais said softly.

"My son is most interested in it." He added.

"What is our common interest?" Fernandez inquired.

"Welfare," he said, "Your daughter has captured my son's mind and his concentration, so I, his father got involved in his welfare."

"How did he do that without my permission?" Ferandes replied.

"Something called "love at first sight;" it is exceptional." Dais said boldly.

" My son likes your daughter and wants to settle down." He added.

"What is your son a soldier or farmer? "The man inquired.

"He is neither a farmer nor a soldier. "Dais replied.

"Then I will not accept your proposal." He replied boldly,

"Before you reject my proposal, I request you listen, my son is a landlord, a business man engaged in dealing with rent, credit, sale of milk, vegetables etc. I assure you your daughter will be happy with him." Dais convinced him.

"Assurance"

"Bring him in front I want to see him." The man demanded.

Anthony went back to the carriage and told his nervous boy to follow him. Nicholas got down from the carriage, and followed his father and then both stood before the handicap man called Fernandez who touched and examined him, at last he patted him on his back. He had heard a lot about Anthony Dais and liked his proposal.

"I found a suitable boy, come inside." He said, They entered the house to discuss the proposal, Lizzy smiled, ran into the bedroom of the house. Both parties agreed to get Nicholas and Lizzy married within two months.

In the battle of First World War in France millions of men were ordered to march forward through trenches built along the long border of northern France, as troops rushed forward, many were shot and injured, lakhs were killed. During this war Indian soldiers had to save themselves from German machine gun fire, thousands were wounded and sent home. Fernandez was a soldier injured on the leg and sent home.

—— **Chapter no14**

— **The Dais family**

1912 Nicholas Dias and Lizzie married and settled at Kalina, Santacruz where his father Anthony Dais, Zamindar (or Landlord) owned vast tracks of land and other properties like fruits gardens full of coconuts, tamarind targollas, betel nuts jackfruits, jambuls, mangoes and other types of tropical fruits trees and paddy fields. The landlord employed laborers and cultivated rice, vegetables fruits trees, they also reared domesticated animals like buffalo's cows, goats, poultry and horses, each animal had a shed. Many laborers employed in dairy business and in agricultural. Both businesses were running smooth. The family prospered in their business and was happy. Family owned a large chawls given on rent, maintained horse carriages and reared many horses tied in the open or inside the shed. At the same time, their pawn business was also doing well, the villagers pawned their properties and gold with them. This family was rich and famous in Santa Cruz and Kurla.

The Kalina village situated close to Mithi river, either side of it consisted of open fields, forest and other open land, further down covered with mangroves. This river originated from the Tansa and Vihar lakes, like a snake flowed into the Mahim bay where it met the sea.

 The villagers travelled to Kurla church to fulfill their religious needs as there was none here.

Anthony heard people cry, donated land and money, built new church, it saved their travelling time.

As the years passed by four daughters were born, the first daughter was named Dolly, then Luisa, Doris and Ivy. The couple was sad that they had no son, heir to their estate, prayed and prayed for a son.

God gave them a son Sunny, later on two more daughters name Jessie and Eunice.

Anthony died and the entire estate came to only son Nicholas, the heir to the Dais's throne.

When eldest daughter Dolly was in her youth, Nicholas found a soldier and married her off, gave them land and money, the couple settled at Marol.

Other three daughters were still below eighteen, so they were left to be married later.

   1930.

Karl Max wrote Das Capital and knew the return on

capital would be better than return on wages. The capitalist would grow rich and get richer and with his wealth he would control many industries, just by investing in it.

The capitalist knew how to calculate his real net worth as on date, he first added interest amount to his initial capital investment, subtracted inflation rate that damaged his net worth and deducted all expense, added net profit from his running business. He employed his capital in different sectors and became wealthier.

After their initial success in cotton trade, Tata ventured into cotton mills, steel and hotels so on, this group owned many enterprises. From cotton cloth, steel to soap etc this group was running and controlling many companies, thus you can say they had a finger in every pie. Before the remote control was invented, the capitalist knew how to remote control his empire, by putting choice of his men in control of his estate with limited power if the manager did not perform as per expectation he could be fired.

This Big gun with huge money and material possessions, the affluent and fastidious Tata was still unhappy, whenever he looked up at the sky, he regretted that birds could fly but he could not? If he did not possess the natural wings like them, he could acquire artificial wings and fly. This man-made bird needed large tract of land to remove the drag and fly. While the same aircraft descended again it took long drive to stop, long runway and other sheds were needed.

To build an airport, large tracts of land is needed, at that time there was lot and lots of vacant land in Bombay but consisted of paddy fields, forest, not salt pans and shallow sea mangroves land which had to be reclaimed from sea bed. Tata wanted flat and stable land, without much delay to build an airport. He also wanted a quick solution to his ambition of starting a new airline in India, no wasting time and large sum of money to reclamation of land. Tata group was influential and well connected with the British government, persuaded them to acquire the fields, flat and stable land i.e. the agricultural land from Santa Cruz to Andheri and Kurla in Bombay under land acquisition act of 1894.

Already British had connected India peninsular from west to east and north to south by rail, main roads, establish English education system and courts, civil service. What the British wanted from the subjects, to suppress their mind to make them obedient and follow them, the result was opposite reaction, it had awakened Indians mind to demand full freedom.

The railway, post office system and common English language, helped and connected these culturally diverse people who spoke more than four hundred fifty different languages, to find a common language of communication, people to people. That was the greatest achievement of English language, it united the people with each other and for particular cause to demand full freedom from English rule.

British wanted India to remain under develop nation subject to English rule. They were also not keen to develop air travel but the American revolt against British rule, awaken the educated Indians also. The freedom struggle was on, now and then there were strikes at many places throughout India, Mahatma Gandhi disobedience movement and resentment to British rule, had weakened the British Empire. These freedom fighters staged more and more demonstrations everywhere, it frightened them.

 When Tata airport proposal came to the table, they thought fast air travel is essential, we must to suppress this freedom movement.

The happenings in Germany and other places in Europe after 1930 made them realize air travel is must to fight the Germans, so, the British entertained Tata request and the permission was granted to acquire land.

The advertisements were put in the newspapers as announcements to acquire land for the airport and the collector sent notices to land owners to vacate their own land and they would be paid compensation as Government rule.

They also sent men beating the big brass plates and drums in the villages to make the land acquisitions announcements.

 The proposal to build an airport on their land was approved by the government and kept as a secret. It did not even consult land owners putting the advertisements or before making these announcements to acquire their land, so many landowners were in the dark or not aware of the purpose?

"There is lot of vacant land available in Bombay, why take away the fertile land?" people thought.

The people, landowners and laborers protested and pleaded their case before the collector as it was concerned with their livelihood and survival.

People never understood sudden change in land use from agriculture to airport, traumatized and helpless. At last police force was sent to vacate the agricultural land.

The landowners the original inhabitants of Bombay called East Indian, generation after generation had cultivated this land, agriculture was the only source of livelihood known to them. When this resistance failed, it affected the agricultural laborers the most, who not only lost their jobs but also became homeless as they lived on the same land, they were shocked, some committed suicide. The lands were acquired at cheap rates below the prevailing market rate.

Many families of Sahar, Kalina Marol and Kurla for generations after generation, had imitated their parents and followed same occupation taught to them, cultivated of rice, vegetables, fruits and dairy on their land. They not only lost their land but also their livelihood and did not know which way to go. Same was case of the Zamindar, Dais family at Kalina, suddenly their life turned into a blank slate, not knowing where to begin again? Lizzy cried and cried became thin and abruptly died first, within two months her husband Nicolas followed her, leaving their seven children to be on their own, six sisters with only one brother.

At last vast land was acquired at throw price and the work for first airport in Bombay started.

The Tata was happy that it could influence the British government, get license and permission to start a new airline business. It built a runaway on the stable ground that needed less land filling. It saved the cost of land reclamation if it was shallow sea, mangrove land that was plenty all over the Mithi River and the coast line. This capitalist was more concerned about building the airport fast, the need of hour to acquire land for the artificial bird to land and takeoff. The aircraft purchased and his ambition is fulfilled, to fly, this aircraft a became a show piece, his strength, his dream had come true.

What about the people and the laborers who lost their land and of their livelihood?

------Chapter no 15~~3~~

------ **Change of life style**

This sudden and unexpected action left Zamindar Dais family at center of four cross roads, not knowing which road to take? Both parents died of shock, the children were left in mourning and the old recollections haunted them, and the girls found something was missing in the house, left it and lived at their aunt's place. Sunny fourteen years old, only male heir took over the business and was compelled to play his father role, lived in the same house with

the servants.

Only son left to manage the remaining estate of the Dais family which consisted of agriculture, dairy and poultry business, plus six tenanted housings and pawn business. Still schooling, he had no practical experience in dealing with this cunning world. His presence was essential, so as supervisor he was engaged in daily routine work in sale of agricultural produce, milk, toddy etc. The rent from the tenanted property and profits from pawn businesses provided some hope. Then he recollected the location of the buried treasure, earthen pots full of Guineas gold coins buried inside the house. His father often pointed his finger and had disclosed this location by before dying. Now the goose that laid golden eggs was in his possession, so he was excited, daily he was busy entertaining his village friends lavishly.

 Sunny was fifth in line of succession, young tall and healthy confident, took over the rein of Dais family. When his sisters returned home, they heard voices and calls, made believed their parents are still alive living in the same house. Sometimes they hallucinated thinking their parents are alive, caught hold of their hand, twisted their ears and guided them, it also slapped them to correct the wrong action taken, all that is still existing, in reality it was missing, so they wept.

In the morning, the servants completed their routine and kept the produce of land in front of their house, dairy workers milked the cows, buffaloes and kept their milk for sale, climbed the coconuts and targollas trees and removed two types of toddies; the thick and the light sweet one called Neera, filled the large earthen jars and kept it for sale.

The supervisor noted the day's produce in his note book and accounted for the sale in the evening.

On weekends English men beaten by taste of the wild flesh, it was a fashion to hunt a wild boar or fowl or deer, frequented the ever-green forest close to the lakes. It was full of different variety of birds and wild animals, their hunting ground and hunter trope was needed to celebrate a Sunday.

 Werner Watts and his group of friends, dressed in shorts, brought trained dogs with them to hunt these wild animals, while the Indian hunters managed it with their long gun, they only fired when the prey was within a given range. A dispute arose between the English and the Indian hunters over use of dogs; the Indians argued with the English not to use dogs as it warned the animal in advance and loss of hunting opportunity. The English in turn protested that it was an innovation over the old Indian way of hunting; this debate resulted in loud mouth fights. After spending the night hunting, in the morning both the parties carried their hunted trophies and usually assembled at the Zamindar Dais's court yard to drink fresh toddy. This fight was amiable settled, as they poured glasses of fresh toddy down their throat. When the mood changed Sunny Dais ordered the servants to serve tea for the English men. While the group enjoyed and his three sisters watched the show from their house windows, giggling and laughing at them.

When the eldest daughter Dolly came of age, she was lucky, parents were alive and got her married to a soldier, they gave them land and money to settle down.

Now Louisa, Doris and Ivy still young were left, not as lucky as Dolly, their parents no more, they took control of their life and moved on, let fate decided what is good for us, they thought, they based their decisions on own intuition and divine providence.

In the morning, four lines of soldiers came marching, accompanied by a major riding the horses, from the Kalina military camp. It was their daily routine practice of drills on the open fields, grass and rough terrain close to their house. When exhausted, after the drill, they rushed at the wells, pulled the buckets, filled with water to wash their faces. Then surrounded the toddy shop close to house to refresh their bodies and minds with Neera glass in hand they boosted, "what a sweet drink, god creation, better than the sweet dish offered at the canteen." Already acquainted with Sunny, they pulled him close and cracked jokes but there was other attraction also his three sisters. Bansi Udawat from Rajasthanwas fascinated by the beauty of the second sister Doris, frequented this place after the drills, fell in love with her; got familiar with family and won her heart. She agreed to his proposal on one condition, this marriage should be solemnized in a Christian manner, so they got married in a church. At the end of fifteen century, five ships with 250 Portuguese sailors arrived as bachelors, anchored near the Bombay coast line. Men in four ships and one ship carried the supplies, so marriages between the locals and the Europeans was common affair, next came the English, a mixed population prevailed in Bombay.

Now Sunny was below twenty, young, suddenly took

over the responsibility of the house and the routine control, of diary and agricultural business, set up by his father. He was busy with running it, along the pawn business and rent collection. In his youth he was also enjoying with his friends in the evening. His time was fully utilized by routine work. After observing his routine life, his mother sister and aunty was worried about the girls in house, would spoil their life, if left alone with Sunny. They decided and took two young sisters Jessie and Eunice, below the age of ten and still schooling. She admitted them in Mount Mary convent; the boarding school at Bandra, the nuns will take better care of them. Werner Watts was in love with a tall fair Luisa, frequented the house, and married her in 1940. He left his family home, rented another home in Bandra. He worked as an officer with the Railways, maintained an English lavish life style and lived with his wife Luisa, spent his weekends at Mahalakshmi race coast, watching horse race and betting on them. Keeping up appearances matter much to him, than the lost or gain on betting, he was happy to follow the English tradition.

A daughter was born Agnes in Bandra, at the peak of the Second World War, he changed his mind, left his job with railways and joined the army, he was sent to the front in Burma to fight the Japanese, spent four years with the army.

Ivy was thin, shy and simple, not interested in wealth and fame, she got married John Shakri also working for the railways. That how the three elder sisters found their own partners and settle down.

——— **Chapter no 164**

———**John finds a partner**

From a life of comfort, with servants and luxury, two younger sisters Jessie and Eunice spent their childhood in distress inside Mount Mary convent school situated on the hill, at Bandra, surrounded with lot of greenery. They were isolated from home life, without parents they left to nuns to care for them, accepted their fate as God plan.

 When Jessie Dais completed her schooling, as per policy of the convent, a mature adult had to be release when she comes of age, the nuns decided to handed over to her elder sister Louisa Watts. She finished her nursing course and worked as a nurse for a reputed hospital in Bombay. Eunice Dais still young was studying in seven standards, left lonely without her elder sister, got bored of the boarding school and isolated life. She requested nuns for release, they pressured her to finish her schooling, she said no and insisted with them to release her soon. So, the nuns did the same to her and left her with elder Louisa to live. Both were fair good looking and strong girls of average heights, fluent in speaking and writing English. Soon Eunice secured a clerk job at the Uniliver ltd soap factory at Sewrcc in Bombay. Unable to bear the odder of the soap manufacturing process, she left her job, after some months she joint Crompton greaves as a clerk. John was twenty-five years old, care free man. His parents both were earning members, made enough money and took care of household expense; they ignored his contribution. Still his youth, free to enjoyed life. he spent evening and holidays with a group of his friends, which had assembled in separate room of a bungalow close by, on evenings and holidays, they loved music, travelling and tasted different types of drinks.

 After work John frequented the grounds of biggest church and school in Bandra called Saint Peter church, it has large open areas, for children to play jockey and football and other games as they pleased. His sister Flory and her friends also here came to relax in the evening. During their daily meetings here, John was introduced to Eunice by his sister; she was youngest daughter of Nicholas Dais the Zaminder. She studied up to seven standard and was released from the convent by nuns and handover to the care her elder sister Luisa Watts, John was 26 years old; it was time to settle down. He courted and married her in1950.

Chapter no17

Coimbatore connection

~~Virgin place.~~

~~On15th AUGUST 1947 India was like a new born~~

~~baby, like a mother she accepted large inflow of~~

~~refugees from Pakistan and accommodated them at various locations throughout India. In Bombay the British army vacated many military camps along the coast line and many other places, refugees filled in this place.~~

~~During the Second World War India had spent lot of money, manpower and material. Still it had good balance of trade and surplus cash, the economy was not in bad shape but there was severe food shortage and mounting inflation.~~

In1934, **S.K.**Toubro was sent as a consultant by~~Toubro had worked for four years, from1934 to 1938 as consultant and had built~~ F. L. Smidth &co **Denmark,** for constructing **a** new **cement plant in Coimbatore, Madras province, it** had designed and supplied equipment **for it.** He had worked as an adviser **for** this project, for four years, up to 1938 here. **During** ~~to th~~is period of construction and ~~He~~ commission of this cement plant, **which he** had helped to build and **he recognized Tamils** talent, ability in fast execution ~~talent in fast execution~~ **of** this project~~the project.~~

To revenge the capture Fort William **in** Calcutta, by Siraj ud Daulah, Robert Clive of East India company took a force from **Madras, and recaptured** it. Toubro did not conspire like him but~~,~~ ~~he~~ imitated his policy~~wanted~~ of~~to~~ recruit~~ing~~ personnel~~people~~ from Tamil Nadu, so. ~~Now~~ he insisted, L&T purchase office space at Madras, Larsen agreed. In November 1950 Toubro and John visited Madras and purchased office accommodation~~space~~ there, Toubro recruited some personnel ~~people~~ and ~~returned to Bombay.~~ both~~They had~~ purchased new furniture for it. He returned to Bombay~~,~~ and he instructed John to remain there, to supervisor the painting and furnishing of this new office; this was L&T's first branch office outside Bombay.

On 21st January 1951 John received a telegram, "a son is born, come home." He could not leave this work half incomplete, as the furnishing of the branch office was on, it got over in February 1951. He returned home with a basket of fruits and sweets to celebrate his son christening, there was joy and lot of celebrations in the house.

He returned home with a basket of fruits and sweets to celebrate his son christening, there was joy and lot of celebrations in the house, family members looked upon this first-born child with amazement. Even neighbor Jerome Nunes and his wife Mary, now without a grown-up son, who worked and supported them, unfortunately God took him away that lost was unbearable. But seeing a new born John's son named Raymond they were also happy and excited, it gave them some consolation, as they could take care of him as their own son.

As Raymond grew, he daily ~~frequent~~frequents their place, this couple got some relief from sadness playing with him, it made them forget about their great loss after seeing him,- they devoted lot of time to take care of him as if he is their own child. Jerome was a devoted catholic, daily attended the first morning Mass at St Peter church and came back home, had breakfast. At 7 am he removed his drum set, placed above his Burma teak wood decorated cupboard, he set it in front of him and started drumming, the sounds of drum beats, vibrated and reflected throughout neighborhood. As soon as drumming sound hit Raymond's ears, now two years, he awoke and ran from his bed to the neighbor Jerome Nunes house, took the drum sticks from his hands, bang the drums as much as he could and then gave up. The neighbors did not object to Nunes's hobby for they also liked to hear the instrument music.

Jerome worked for the port trust and retired, as a

hobby, ~~he practices~~ playing ~~on side drums and became~~ he was a professional drummer~~.~~ ~~He~~and played for St Paul's band, a well-known band group in the suburbs of Bombay. Founded by him and Lawrence D'mello at Chapel road in Bandra, this band played for weddings, ~~and~~ consorts ~~and church processions.~~

~~As Raymond grew, they devoted lot of time to take care of him carried him and played with him. Jerome daily routine, attended the first morning Mass at St Peter church and came back home, had breakfast. At 7 am he removed the drum set, placed above his Burma teak decorated wooden cupboard, he set it in front of him. As soon as he had placed the drums on the stands, he started drumming, the sounds of drum beats, vibrated and reflected throughout neighborhood, when it hit Raymond's ears, now two years he awoke and ran from his bed to the neighbor Jerome Nunes house, took the drum sticks from his hands and bang the drums as much as he could and then gave up. The neighbors did object to Nunes's hobby for they also liked to hear the sound of his drumming.~~

~~Jerome worked for Bombay port trust and was a professional drummer, he and Lawrence DeMello~~

~~played for St Paul's band, a famous band group in the suburbs, founded by them at Chapel road in Bandra. This band was always engaged by people and played for wedding and consorts, church proces~~**After completing fifty years of service to the Christian community, this band group erected a marble statue of St Paul in front of Mount Carmel Church as a memorial of their band group, it is still there.**

Jerome had other interest of fishing, boating, swimming in shallow sea in the Bay of Mahim, close to the sea shore along Bazar and Chapel roads near his house, during summer months from March to June, when sea was calm, and the tide came and filled the shallow sea twice a day, ~~where~~ **he would cut banana trunks from the fields and built two three floats, for children to hold and learn swimming, under his guidance and directions, he taught Raymond** ~~at very early age five~~ **and other neighborhood children, the initial art of swimming that how Raymond learnt swimming at very early age five.**

~~Even his neighbor Jerome Nunes and his wife Mary were happy to see John's new born child, this couple~~

~~had a grown-up son, who worked and supported~~

~~them, unfortunately God took him away, now~~

~~without a child, they were relied to see John's new~~

~~born son named Raymond and considered him as t~~

~~Before 1938 Toubro had worked as cement plant~~

~~consultant in Madras province and had recognized~~

~~Tamils talent, ability in fast execution of the cement~~

~~plant project, he wanted to recruit people from~~

~~Tamil Nadu. In 1950, he insisted L&T purchase~~

~~office space in Madras city, Larsen agreed. Toubro~~

~~and John visited Madras and purchased office space~~

~~there; Toubro recruited some people and returned to~~

~~Bombay. From November 1950 till February 1951~~

~~John remained there, to supervisor the furnishing of~~

~~this new office; it was L&T's first branch outside~~

~~Bombay.~~

~~On 21st January 1951 he received a telegram, "a son~~

~~is born, come home." He could not leave this work~~

~~half incomplete, as the furnishing of the branch~~

~~office was still on, it got over in February 19~~**He**

returned home with a basket of fruits and sweets to

celebrate his son christening, there was joy and lot of

celebrations in the house, family members looked

upon this first-born child with amazement. Even

neighbor Jerome Nunes and his wife Mary now

without a grown-up son, who worked and supported them, unfortunately God took him away, lost was unbearable, they were also happy but seeing a new born John's son named Raymond which gave them some consolation as their own son.

 As Raymond grew, he daily frequent their place, this couple got some relief from sadness about their great loss after seeing him play, they devoted lot of time to take care of him as if he is their own child. Jerome was a devoted catholic, daily attended the first morning Mass at St Peter church and came back home, had breakfast. At 7 am he removed his drum set, placed above his Burma teak wood decorated cupboard, he set it in front of him and started drumming, the sounds of drum beats, vibrated and reflected throughout neighborhood. As soon as drumming sound hit Raymond's ears, now two years, he awoke and ran from his bed to the neighbor Jerome Nunes house, took the drum sticks from his hands, bang the drums as much as he could and then gave up. The neighbors did not object to Nunes's hobby for they also liked to hear the instrument music.

Jerome worked for the port trust, he was a professional drummer and played for St Paul's band, a well-known band group in the suburbs of Bombay. Founded by him and Lawrence D'mello at Chapel road in Bandra, this band played for wedding and consorts.

When this band group completed fifty years of service to the Christian community in Bombay, they erected a marble statue of St Paul in front of Mount Carmel Church as a memorial of their band group, it is still there. He had other interest of fishing in shallow sea in the Bay of Mahim where he taught Raymond at very early age five and other neighborhood children the initial art of swimming.

~~India being an agricultural economy, where ever it lacked basic infrastructure like roads, railways, seaports/airports it wanted to make up, plus many basic industries. For this Planning Commission presented the draft outline of the First Five Year Plan for the period April 1951 to March 1956, to the parliament in Dec. 1952.~~

~~Objectives of First Five-Year Plan:~~

~~(i) To increase food production, so it gave the highest priority to agriculture to overcome the food crisis and to curb inflation.~~

~~(ii) To fully utilizes available natural resources like~~

iron ore etc, it built steel plants and to utilizes water resources of the country, it built hydro electric dams to produce electricity,

(v) To build economic overheads such as roads, railways, irrigation, power, etc.

(vi) To reduce inequalities in income and wealth.

Outlay:

The total proposed outlay was Rs. 3,870 crore of which 44.6% of the total public sector outlay was devoted to development work.

Assessment:

India's First Five-Year plan achieved success in many fields, in many cases, the plan targets were exceeded.

(a) Although the target for national income growth was only an 11% increase, the actual increase was 18% from Rs. 8850 crore the national income increased to Rs. 10,480 crore by the end of the first plan. Per capita income went up by 11%.

(b) Food production rose from 52.2 million tonnes in 1951-52 to 65.8 million tonnes in 1955-56, whereas the plan target was only 61.6 million tonnes. In cotton, jute, sugarcane and oilseeds, the achievements were close to the targets.

(c) Industrial production increased during the plan

~~period. Production of mill-made cloth and locomotives exceeded the plan targets. Many new industries like oil refining, ship-building, aircraft, railway, were established during the plan.~~

~~(d) During the plan period, there was an increase of about 33% in the number of students attending primary schools. A sum of Rs. 101 crore was spent on health services, and a large number of hospitals and dispensaries were opened.~~

~~(e) During this period, the railway system was strengthened. 380 miles of new lines were added. 430 miles of lines which were dismantled during the Second World War was restored. Highways were increased by 636 miles with 30 major bridges and there was improvement of 4000 miles of existing roads.~~

~~(f) It stabilized the inflationary pressure on the economy. as the agricultural sector increased food production,~~

The country's first five-year plan provided more opportunities for L&T, collaboration with Caterpillar Tractor USA proved very successful and right decision taken, there was big demand for earth moving equipment, spares and service, L&T signed big deals for purchase and leasing of these items with

other construction companies that needed these items for evacuation, levelling of ground work, like big hydroelectric dams' projects etc. It became a separate division itself, it learnt from this company about earth moving machines and its maintenance, service spares, specialized in it. Later it also purchased design specifications and started manufactured the same type of equipment in India. India being an under develop country, offered more scope for its sister concern ECC also to engage in engineering & construction of new projects. ECC quoted for new projects and gave L&T orders for caterpillar items, used in development of infrastructure, like roads bridges etc basic and heavy industries like iron and steel plants, large dams for electricity. When L&T quoted for heavy industries or for specialized large projects. It put advertisements Indian engineers but found that technical education in India was still in infant stage, the searched for engineers continued, but they were rare commodity. Since it could not find them, it imported Danish engineers and utilized their service, talent, to design heavy industrial items like blast furnace for steel plants and other complicated projects.

It also purchased technical knowhow from other European companies to manufactured bottle closures, imported some Danish experts to train workers and also signed new collaboration agreements with Europeans companies to manufacture heavy equipment. it started to manufactured new items previously imported here. Now L&T was moving fast, signed collaboration agreements with other reputed European companies and recruited more engineers, continued to develop new products. Thus, the two founders were engaged in diversified activities, determined to see the growth of this group. They had different thoughts, when they found engineers and advisers to accompany them, they gradually moved away from John. Now these professionals made many changes, some showed off their book induced knowledge, They implemented division of labor and specialization offered better salary and facilities. They established the personnel department and brought more rules to show off their professionalism, so it became necessary to submit more certificates and give more details as demanded by them. But professionals were not always fair, some were regional minded, recruited their own people from their native place not much educated speak English or trained in trades but some to spy on others employees and reported to them.

The output produce by new work force was small compared to the efforts put in by the initial team of four men. New factory working timings were changed to eight hours duty, it implemented labor laws and the worker's union came in existence, now for extra work, workers were paid ~~overtime, strong~~overtime, strong union forth for their rights and their service was made permanent.

What about extra hours that John and William had put in service of this child, since inception? Where was no time limit and no union to fight for their rights?

In that small room at Nicole Street, Ballard estate, Bombay, when Larsen was seated inside, Toubro stood outside near the door, wondering about getting some business and how will L&T survive without a job in hand?

When Second World War was on, no one was willing to offer (food for this hungry child). L&T was starving for work to survive, two men (William and John) performed many different types of jobs, big or small without complaining, had also resolved to make this baby walk. It was with their dedication, cooperation and coordination, this newly born child lived.

That time there was no such thing as "my time is over, or eight hours are over or this is not my job." When the factories were established, things were segregated, system routine was based on division of labor, the employee's attitude changed, I am recruited for particular job only or that is not my job and I will do the work only for eight hours per day only, which I am skilled worker, why should I go out or do for other job. William and John's motive was, to do whatever they could to make this start up survive, and their untiring efforts and fighting spirit, kept it moving.

For new comers, division of labor made things easy, work was segregated and it became a routine and workers mostly performed given work only, argued and pointed out their fingers to others." my time is over" or that is not my job" and the professionals agreed with them.

In the past to make L&T stand on its two legs, John did not think about it, he considered every work or task was contributing towards the progress of the company. L& T and John worked seriously and cooperated in all matters of the company with only one motto "In service lies success," It was their dedication, hard work and ideas that transformed this small firm into a reputed one.

When L&T's factory was established; making some profits, so called professionals managers opened their eyes wide, came begging. Now L&T looked very attractive, like a beautiful young girl in a ready to marry bargain bazaar. L&T recruited more and more people, they roamed around founders became close to them.

When the buffet was laid on the table, professionals behaved like hungry lions, forgot about the people that had put in many efforts to prepare this buffet and lay it on the table for them. The managing team got up from its sleep and realized that John's qualification is a civil draftsman, so they placed him in the architectural dept and forgot about his contributions.

During those most difficult and uncertain times of the Second World War, the professionals after peeping into L&T's small room that could hardly fit one table, ran away. Only the humble John and William kept faith and worked hard, L&T relied on practical experience and commonsense, it survived.

John believed L&T had expertise in diversified fields of engineering and would make tremendous progress and it did, made more progress, it became a super star in the field of advance engineering. Now in this mad rush where was his rank? He remained humble, unknown for his initials contributions for he did not believe in name and fame

L&T was the pioneer in India, in design, manufacture and in installation of complete dairy plants, for milk processing and manufacturing of milk products. It worked hand in hand with National dairy development board(NDDB) and played a very important role in development of dairy industry in India. Milk cooperatives societies helped in collection of milk from farming communities, spread far and wide in a state i.e. procurement side. To establish dairy plants, L&T was the consultant, it also designed and built high speed bottling plants to supply clean milk to large cities, this helped the Gujarat state cooperatives to establish "Amul" brand in India. NDDB launched called "Operation Flood 1 and 2" for betterment of milk collection from rural farming community at fair price.

As L&T, being qualified engineers did not believe in

wasting Time and Talent for mad Hitler who had pride with wrong ideas of capturing whole Europe. They devoted time to different types of civil mechanical electrical instrumentation projects, L&T manufactured and fabrication of heavy machinery for dairy cement helped India's industrial development. L&T had gained experienced in many different fields of engineering, fabrication and manufacturing, it diversified, L&T set up design departments and employed many engineers, designs large and heavy engineering products, precision machineries, spares for need for nuclear plants, like pressure vessels, heat exchangers, calandrias etc and fabricates it.

L&T was the big brother and ECC (engineering construction corporation ltd) born before L&T in 1944 considered herself as small sister, who always supported her big brother in construction and executing of the projects that were secured by her brother.

1936 Larsen had secured a big contract from Tata group for three new cement plants for F.L.Smidth, Denmark but Hitler banned exports, so this company could not fulfil the contract, these plants were diverted to Germany. He was helpless, still maintained contacts with ACC house at Churchgate, Bombay, he had many Parsee friends in the city, some also worked with the company. Thus he came in contact with Dr Homi Bhabha, chairman of atomic energy commission. Who visited Powai works, saw the set up it had engineers, modern design room heavy fabrication and ECC did completely contract job?

In 1964 L&T & ECC both combined and secured order to build India first nuclear plant which was constructed at Trombay in Bombay.

Import substitute

 L&T executed vast varieties of diversified projects in dairy, cement, steel, hydroelectric dams, petroleum refineries etc it designed, manufactured or modified products thus made them suitable for Indian condition which were previously imported, saved foreign exchange for the country.

 Success made them think India is better place to settle, they lived in Bombay and work made them to travel to different parts of India. They found Indians are intelligent, friendly and hard working people, they understood Indian way of life, Indian culture, its people and its diversity in dress, customs and languages. They got used to their work culture, simple Indian way of life, they also understood Indians treat them their guess and respected them, this made them feel India is their second home. Their partnership was based understanding and cooperation; from beginning they realized, good team work is necessary for this company to survive; each player must be sincere, hardworking, cooperate, must believe and trust each other. As chairman of the board of directors they cooperated shared the responsibilities of this company equally. When Larsen was absent Toubro took it over easily, as both were familiar with the work, how this company functions, they took responsibility. were flexible and believed in democracy, for they always debated before execution of the job.

" Time," was the most precious commodity of their life, not to be wasted, but utilize it carefully, given jobs, appointments must be honored in time. During the monsoon, heavy rains flooded the streets life came to stand still in Bombay and traffic stopped, less attendance at work, work disrupted, they took leave alternately, they went to Denmark to spend their holidays.

Displaced by war in 1938, they found home and settler in Bombay and India offered work and opportunities in their field of expertise, for the engineers.

"L&T from the outset has been a company with the object of establishing trade, commerce and manufacturing by and for the people of India." Larsen commented.

When L&T was small, unknown firm and looking for work during the war, it found it difficult to get consultancy jobs. It was war time, no new companies or new works were not coming up, it faced uncertain future. Since its inception, it always wanted to be unique, to face competition and survive.

_________Chapter no_18 ~~16~~

Common hobbies

As India made progress, lot of changes took place, and new opportunities opened in different fields of engineering, instrumentation, heavy fabrication of straight drums for oil refineries, cement/ fertilizer plants. L&T since its inception, always wanting to be ahead of time in any new fields, be it engineering, or nuclear energy, first quoted for projects, then when it needed technical collaboration, it consulted foreign firms cooperated, designed and executed projects in India, many first-time new projects in India through its own in-house experience or foreign collaboration. Whether it was prepared or not, it took chances or challenges to make in India what was not done previously. It ventured into new areas of engineering, construction, manufacturing and other fields like construction of nuclear plants, which were untouched before. L&T sought collaboration or purchased drawings or brought in technical experts from aboard thus managed its projects.

Bad times did not last long, but persons with strong will and determination did survive.

As time by, its reputation and brand became famous, more opportunities opened up for the company, with success came the desire for L&T to live in India. Before 1956, Mallet Bunder near Dockyard Bombay was head office of L&T and ECC, the accounts and other office, administration work was also carried at here and Powai works, two places were separated by big distance.

Mallet Bunder is situated near the dock area, crowded with heavy traffic of trucks, out and in movement from here, to other places, traffic movement is obstructed and slow, which made it think of a larger place, where all the board members, accounting and other works could be done at one place.

L&T with more business in hand, found its own cars had increased and there was less parking space here. It is also I channels, asbestos roof shed, not sufficient, the company had grown and expanded it needed bigger place.

L&T decided that everything should be at one place, back to Ballard Estate, from where it started, had a small one room office previously before 1944 Bombay dock fire.

It first rented the ICI house at Ballard estate for

some time, and then purchased it.

From top floor of this office building, they again got view of the shipping activities inside Bombay port and the surrounding sea, it is here that L&T had spent its time during the war, port area was nostalgic place, the recollections remained and were refreshed by observing the dock activities again.

Larsen, Toubro and John had some common interest, to do new things, be it craft work or manufacturing of new product or machinery, then to learn and acquire new knowledge from it, ~~do new things, be it craft work or manufacturing of new product or machinery~~.

Another common interest was to travel and see new places, and the ~~and experience different types of weather conditions,~~ natural environment surrounding them, evolution in different variety of life forms like fishes' birds' animals i.e. they loved the creation and wanted to see as much as possible, in their one life time ends. Also to experience different types of weather conditions.

Next t~~T~~hese three persons, ~~also~~ loved to live near the sea, although Larsen lived in south Bombay near Beach Candy, he loved and appreciated the quite calm atmosphere of Juhu Island, with~~,~~ the long clean seashore, sea breeze, full of coconut trees, cool climate, bungalows situated close to sea. Backyard of a bungalow inside the compound, ~~full of coconut trees,~~ with sea view in front, Larsen ~~where he~~ hired a space. Requested L&T architectural department to ~~A~~ ~~specially~~ design special wooden hut for him, a beautiful spacious hut was constructed and placed here. Where he loved to spend, most of his weekends ~~there~~ and enjoying the sea breeze.

In the Bay of Mahim close to seashore, near Bandra town market, John's house is situated, two houses away was the sea shore, where sea water kissed it and travelled back with tide twice a day. With the tide came the waves roaring waves, sea water, filled the large circular shallow bay area near Bazar and Chapel roads.

The sail boats filled with building sands also came with it, from Vasai creek these boats came and floated outside the bay, when tide filled the shallow sea area, these boats entered along with it inside and waited for their turn to unload the sand at Mahim Rearty bunder, (sand dock).
By this time, the tide retreated two miles away from the seashore, the sail boats and fishing boats were stranded in the shallow water or sea sand wherever

they were located.

Before 1975, Juhu and Versova were two islands, with Arabian Sea in front, the back sides consisted shallow sea areas, covered with the large mangrove forest. Separated from the main land, they were only connected by single roads, it was a one-way street, only single roads connectedto and from -these two islands to Bombay.

John lived close to the Bay of Mahim but he also treasured the calm atmosphere of Versova island, filled with evergreen forest especially coconuts trees and clean long beach in front, bungalows situated along the sea shore, with a fishing village situated at one end of it.

The old fishing village and the fisherfolks maintained their tradition way of life, deep rooted in Indian culture, for generation after generation, their main occupation is fishing. From far from outside, this island looked like a man's head, whose hairs consisted of coconuts trees, the land was fertile and vegetables were cultivated, there were also fruit gardens full of coconuts, targola, mango, tamarind, chickoo flowers trees.

Before 1947, Before 1947 British had built and maintained many military camps, at many places within the Bombay state, mostly along the sea coast, for troops to live and defend this island.~~, located~~

At Versova, ~~along the sea coast of Bombay, for troops to live.~~ these camps ~~were built~~were located, far apart from~~and~~ each other, ~~camp was~~ a ground floor structure, each camp shed consisted of five or six apartments, each apartment had two large rooms, with attached kitchen and separate toilet. With big open place in front for individuals' gardens.

In 1941, after Japan attracted Pearl Harbor, in Pacific Ocean, the British feared a similar type attack here, so all military camps were put on high alert.

IIn 1947 partition of India took place, the British left and ~~the camps were~~ these camps were deserted at many places in Bombay, ~~hundreds of refugees took place and people~~ from Sind and Punjab provinces of Pakistan were brought here and were settled in these vacant camps. ~~came to India and hundreds of refugees were settled in these camps.~~

The Versova island was thinly populated place, with bungalows situated along seashore, farms and lot of green surroundings.

The Second World War ended, soldiers returned

back to their hometown, Luisa's husband Werner Watts came home from Burma, with lot of baggage, consisting his personal and military items, photographs, binocular, camera etc were displayed in the round wooden showcase,~~frame~~ with transparent glass ~~showcase~~ at home. For some personnel reason, he insisted that Bandra is not safe place to stay for him~~, for personal~~.

 In the fifties Luisa and Warner Watts rented a two-room apartment in a military camp situated close to main road, from housing board, opposite the Machlimar bus stop, in Versova island.

This bus stop was called Machlimar (catch fish in Marathi language) as lot and lot of fishes were found swimming close to seashore, in shallow sea water and boats full, varieties of fishes were caught near the seashore. ~~A boat carried this net and it ferried it, fifteen or twenty meters from the sea shore into the sea., encircling the shallow seawater with long rectangular net and two ends attached two long ropes.~~ A boat carried this net and it ferried it, fifteen or twenty meters from the sea shore into the sea. ~~Then it laid in circular way into the seawater covering a half circle area, the fishermen jumped into water, pulled it close to the by seashore.~~

Opposite to their camp, across the road there was a large compound with a big one-story Bungalow called Master bungalow, it belonged to Paymaster a Parse man. It was used as a picnic cottage, full of guests on weekends, they were seen, roaming, eating, drinking and dancing enjoying their weekend here.

 It had semicircle garden in front with a big mango tree in the center, with chickoo trees on side of it, round well near the main entrance of the compound and watchman cabin near the entrance gate. Along the compound wall of this bungalow there were many fully grown coconut trees.

John with his family spent their weekends here. Rising early in the morning, he first went for a walk along the deserted road and then came home for tea, after breakfast, he moved to the abandoned seashore, to observe the fisher men catching fish close to the beach.

He was later joined by his wife and two sons, who brought empty containers to place the fishes.

 Those days' shoals of fishes were found swimming close to the seashore. Fishermen used, a tradition method of fishing, i.e. a long rectangular net called Pera with long ropes, attached two ends of it, carried it a long net called Pera in a small boat, it is large enough, to encircle a small portion of the water sea close to the beach.

Two or three men in a boat, carried this net and went into the sea, ~~a~~After estimating the catch in the shallow water, close to seashore, they dropped the net into sea water, encircling a semi-circle area. It became a circular trap for the fishes in the shallow sea, then fishermen jumped into waist deep water and pulled it on either side, pulling it close to the seashore.

They ~~y gave one end of the net to~~pulled the two ~~with other~~ends of the net, and ~~inside the boat~~ moved it, throu~~wing it into~~gh the sea water, ~~when the whole area was circled, second man threw remaining net into the sea and jumped into it.~~m More men joined in at the two ends and pulled it towards the seashore. As the net with two ends moved, close to the seashore, the sea water receded and~~until~~ the whole catch moved~~was pulled~~ with it. It brought shoals of fishes, trapped closer to the beach, struggling to survive, jumped up into the air, making many attempts to save their lives.

Now it was our time, to move close to approaching waves that brought a variety of fishes, struggling to survive, dancing front of us~~.,~~ Wwe stood in midst of this survival drama, foundwith fishes jumping up, some pounding on our bodies, still we. sStood in the way of this large catch, each person caught some, ran and placed it in the vessels filled with some sea water placed on the dry sand, then ran back to sea, to catch more and back to the dry sand to place the catch. When this game was over, we went to see the catch, fishes are alive and dancing inside vessls again.

In the morning, this beach was mostly empty, in this game of fishing, mostly we were the only family without any competition to catch fish. The fishermen did not object to it, as their catch was always large and their small boat could not accommodate it all. Again, marvelous shoals of fishes were found swimming close to the seashore and again the fishermen laid the trap of round tripping the catch;(shoals of fishes swimming close to the seashore) were trapped in the same net, called perda in Marathi like round Indian milk sweet.

After the fishing adventure was over, it was for bazaar shopping in the Versova village. We mostly walked to the fish market two miles distance; two bus stops away. Sometimes we waited to catch the bus in time, were fortunate for it, those days frequency bus service was after interval one half an hour. This whole island was thinly populated and oversupply of fishes far exceeded the demand here, so it was sent to other places, also there was no ice factory or cold storage facilities available here, hence fish was sold cheap here, market displayed wide variety of fishes, crabs, lobsters etc,. Locally grown vegetables and locally reared stock of hens, sheep was plenty, so mutton was also cheap.

After buying our requirements, we went to known fisher man house, for fresh toddy, drank some and carried some to the home. When we reached home, we found an old car parked near the camp, uncle Vacha and his friends had also joined in for the week end picnic, old friends of Werner Watts from Bandra.

In the evening, we carried the Kodak box camera and the British military binocular with us, all went to the beach. We shot some photos, got closer view of the surroundings, with Mudh island at one end and Juhu beach at the other end.

Those days this beach was neat and clean place, to relaxed and play on the sea sand, children found small light brown crabs, fast running on the sand, gave a chase, I and my brother did the same thing, we tried to catch one but we did not succeed, they moved fast deep inside the sand holes, spread everywhere along the sea shore. We tried another trick to fill these crabs' holes with hot sea sand, to trace their passage of crab hole end and then to catch the crab, we failed to find the correct way after digging.

Short cut to the Juhu beach.

A river separated Versova island from the Juhu island, d~~D~~uring the incoming ~~low~~ tide, sea water rushed behind these inlands from both the sides which had river mouths, into the vast tracks of mangroves lands that stretched from Santa Cruz to Malad and~~which had~~ encircled them from behind. When same tide retreated ~~ff~~arom the back into sea, it rushed from these river mouths outlets, ~~from the vast tracks of mangroves that stretched from Santa Cruz to Malad~~ to ~~sea in~~ front of these islands. ~~A river separated Versova island from the Juhu island.~~ Some people took a chance to cross this river, as a short cut to reach Juhu, ~~them~~ instead of long round journey from Andheri to it. ~~Juhu or~~ Both ends of these islands there was~~Versova.~~ v~~V~~ast open sand beds, one mile away from them. When tide to receded through this river from behind, ~~wo ends of these islands~~it came rushing like wild river water and went into the main sea.

This river crossing was known as the sinking sand area, as the incoming tide came with big waves and outgoing tide, the sea water current rushed back fast, shifted the sand and it loosen river bed that was danger of sinking inside loosen ground. ~~that surrounded both these islands rushed back fast with the current of tide, taking the sand with it.~~

Those days it was a short cut to Juhu beach, but few locals dared to cross it,

Once John told Eunice to stay at her sister place and then take the bus to their home in Bandra, he took his elder son Raymond with him and walked along Versova beach, when they came to the end of it, they stopped. John surveyed the shallow river basin, found the narrow portion of the river flow and saw a man crossing it. He recollected that he had crossed it many times from the same spot.

Tide had retreated but close to the river, the running sea water was still furious, John caught hold of his son hand and moved cautiously, sinking one step at a time in the running river water, they manage to cross it.

From one end of Juhu beach, they walked and after walking some time, along the sea shore, they came close the place where Larsen spent his weekends, in a wooden hut designed by L&T architectural dept where John now worked.

"Look there, that's Larsen's hut, he spends his Sundays here." John said to his son.

"Oh, he also loves the sea." Raymond replied.

Before 1980 Juhu was still clean place with natural surrounding and a long beach.

~~late seventies~~As the Bombay city's population increased, many hotels and buildings were built near the seashore, the Juhu beach became more and more~~was~~ crowded and it lost ~~lost~~ its olds -charms. Larsen loved the quit and clean atmosphere of the old Juhu island, when bungalows with big compounds were replaced by hotels and housing, he was sad to find noise that disturb his peace. So, he shifted to a bungalow at Aksa beach at Mudh island and spent his weekends here, it was also designed by same Architectural dept.

In 1946, when L&T's first survey group, consisting of three founding members i.e. Larsen, Toubro and John visited Powai lake, to find a location for first factory, Danish men were amazed, to see the varieties of trees, birds and wild animals, all that natural habitat, a huge area of evergreen forest within the city's range.

Since 1938 Larsen had lived on this island of good life, surrounded by sea, up to 2003. Seen this master piece of creation, consisting of forest, birds and animals that had existed without hinderance for generations on it.

Then the same environment getting degraded, year after year, by factories, buildings, slums and other activities, many types of life, plants birds' animals, became extinct.

Though he was a busy man, still he devoted time to save, as a trustee of wild life fund India and tried his best to save the remaining natural habitat, the national park area the forest the home of wild creatures of the island of Bombay. He was also the trustee of Royal Bombay Yacht club.

Chapter 19

Recollections don't die soon.

During the fifties and sixties, Toubro rented and lived in Actor Dev Anand's bungalow at Pali Hill, near Carter road, Bandra, also situated close to sea. Those days Pale hill filled with greenery, was lonely and quiet place, occupied by the bungalows, belonging to Bollywood stars, who lived here with their families.

In 1944 Engineering Construction Corporation Limited was established at Mallet Bunder, Dockyard, Bombay, this place is located the dock and it was brought from Bombay port trust after L&T got first contract of making merchant ships self-defence themselves. It gave them hope and confidence of better tomorrow, then they became more serious, to get finance to establish a factory setup, the idea of first modern factory setup was conceived here.

 Toubro was always fond of his friend John Gonsalves, with whom he loved to work, talk and joke, sometimes he shared his feelings about the company and the affairs of world with him.

 Many times, Toubro invited John for cup of tea at

his residence, both joked and recalled their good old days.

Occasionally he and John went for walk down the hill near Petit school, where was open place, a common golf for all, and chatted for a long time, for he loved to talk with him.

Larsen kept in touch with John by exchanging season greetings and also invited him for cup of tea once or twice a year at his residence near Beach Candy.

 Since 1934'Toubro had spent three decades in India, he first was deputed as a consultant, on assignment by F.L. Smidth & co to complete the Coimbatore cement plant contract, his time was well spent here. 1936 after winning the biggest contract from Tatas for three new cement plants for F.L. Smidth & co. Larsen went back to Denmark and was surprised, to see the Nazis rule his country, they ban all exports and diverted cement plants and equipment to Germany, to increase its cement production.

Larsen was frustrated, as all his efforts were in vain, his company cannot execute the contract signed with Tatas.

Denmark is misrule by Hitler's men who are cruel,

insane, don't listen to Danish people, the is compelled him to escape.

Better to take refuge here and be safe.

When Larsen returned to Bombay, he advise Toubro to stay back, better to take refuge here and be safe. Toubro listen to his trusted friend's advice, they took refugestayed back, and remained alive here. ILike hundreds of other Danish, Germans people, who had, deserted their countries and taken refuge here, thus remained alive here, thinking when the war ends, they will return to their native place. They did not waste their time, collaborated and partnership firm came into existence, they struggled to get it moving, luck favored andwith John helped, luck favored L&T to win the tender of M.V. Hilda floating dock, after that there was no looking back.

"The success that came our way, can be attributed to great deal of luck but mainly to our fortune of working with competent and devoted team of four men initially, when there was little hope of this firm becoming successful." Both admitted.

By chance and hard work L&T survived, Toubro also loved India and its culture of pluralism, itn people, it was still a developing country and its standard of living below that of Denmark, it was culturally different and disliked by his grown-up children, who found it difficult to adjust to Indian life style, which they found it to be slow and different from western~~Danish~~ life style. When Toubro children went for further studies in Denmark, his wife also went to live with them, this separation made him think, whether to continue in India or return to his native place.

His children preferred western education and European lifestyle. His children were doing further studies in Denmark and his wife also went to live with them. At last he found himself lonely without his family, in 1963 he decided it was enough, he quit L&T to be with his own family.

 He had already devoted more time of his life, to the company activities in India~~more time~~, many times during his term, he worked overtime, for the company, till late night to get things done or keep them moving, so he devoted more time for the company than for his family.

He ~~left to~~ settled in Denmark but continued as a director L&T and ECC boards up to 1981 then he gave up and died 1983.

He left a foot print, his surname as a trade mark of the company and figured on the name boards, letterheads etc.

 During those hard days of war and uncertainty, they took it easy and faced life as it came. John had the opportunity, not only to work closely with them, they also spent free time with them, they shared personal thoughts with him as they had known him and his character. They believed in humor or laughter was a best medicine that help people forget the past and kept them happy. There was no other better man than John to crack jokes and to laugh with them, they trusted him and found he was free minded, most liberal person who listened to them carefully and understood them. Toubro's recollections remained especially with his family, Larsen and John, also, many persons associated with L&T.

Chapter no 20

L&T's Management style

L&T management style was friendly, both partners were clever, free minded, and open to debates, subject to criticism. They ~~Management style~~ believed in~~was~~ democratic principles, i.e. ~~opened minded,~~ freedom of expression, discussion~~, debate~~ before implementation of an idea.

During free time they accepted jokes and cracked some, to relief themselves from past worries, maintain a joyful mood, laughter was a better medicine.

When L&T was small, unknown firm and looking for work during the war, it found it difficult to get consultancy jobs. It was war time, no new companies or new works were coming up, it faced uncertain future. Since its inception, it always wanted to be unique, to face competition and survive

L&T always wanted to learn, pursue new ideas or techniques to keep up with time or to face competition, to produce better products or new machines or execute new projects as the market demanded. They visited exhibitions or fairs organized and arranged by advanced European countries, observed new products on displays, discussed collaborations, then manufactured the same here. Similar pattern was followed to manufacture import substitutes, based on own knowledge, or research. L&T created many of them, not only in dairy machinery but in many engineering fields and other products,

it saved lot of foreign exchanged for India.

When company grew and became large and more diversified, liberty was given the managing divisional head, in recruitment and promotion and in running the show.

Success made them think India is better place to settle, they lived in Bombay and work made them to travel to different parts of India. They found Indians are intelligent, friendly and hardworking people, they understood Indian way of life, Indian culture, its people and its diversity in dress, customs and languages. They got used to their work culture, simple Indian way of life, they also understood Indians treat them their guess and respected them, this made them feel India is their second home.

Their partnership was based understanding and cooperation; from beginning they realized, good team work is necessary for this company to survive; each player must be sincere, hardworking, cooperate, must believe and trust each other. As chairman of the board of directors they cooperated shared the responsibilities of this company equally.

When Larsen was absent Toubro took it over easily,

as both were familiar with the work, how this company functions, they took responsibility. were flexible and believed in democracy, for they always debated before execution of the job.

" Time," was the most precious commodity of their life, not to be wasted, but utilize it carefully, given jobs, appointments must be honored in time. During the monsoon, heavy rains flooded the streets life came to stand still in Bombay and traffic stopped, less attendance at work, work disrupted, they took leave alternately, they went to Denmark to spend their holidays.

Displaced by war in 1938, they found another home in Bombay and settled here, India offered the engineers, work and opportunities in their field of expertise.

"L&T from the outset has been a company with the object of establishing trade, commerce and manufacturing by and for the people of India." Larsen commented.

.Differentiate

When L&T was small, unknown firm and looking for work during the war, it found it difficult to get business, no new companies or new works were coming up, it was difficult to get business and survive, it faced uncertain future. Since its inception, it always wanted to be unique, to face competition and survive.

 When it was established, believed in free trade and competition and thought,

 "protection is not good, small, big, weak and strong all know how to live and survive in the jungle, same should be the case of the Indian industry."

"I don't really know. But we did adopt a lot of techniques before many others did. We have always believed in democratic management, by merit rather than heredity or contacts, in treating professionals as professionals and in keeping in touch with management institutions to learn new developments and try and incorporate them. "' Larsen commented.

1950/60 Narrow minded

It became, difficult to procure license for building new cement plants, L&T's request for building a small new cement plant to produce more cement was rejected, it harmed the country progress.

"You needed a license to set up even a small factory." Larsen regretted.

 "We used to make 300 tonnes of cement annually

and wanted to double our capacity. The official did not give us the permission." Larsen regretted such type of attitude.

India had few ccment factories with limited capacity that produce

"Cement," basic material of Infrastructure development, the supply could not match the demand, so shortage prevailed and black marketing flourished. Then to the ruling government and the civil servants wanted this sector to remain under their control, license raj prevailed and the politicians and civil servants were not willing to change, and liberate it.

 With this mentality India remained backward, the government in power did not allow free trade, was not much concerned about infrastructure development, hence it was difficult to procure license for building cement plants, so the country's industrial development remained slow.

L&T's request for building a new cement plant to produce more cement was rejected,
"You needed a license to set up even a small factory." Larsen regretted. "We used to make 300 tonnes of cement annually and wanted to double our

capacity. The official did not give us the permission." Larsen said.

 India politicians and civil servants were less concerned about the country progress, industrial progress of the country suffered due to their ignorance, knowing cement was the base or main component of infrastructure development. Hence GDP growth slow down.

Labour relationship and welfare

L&T labor policies were better pay, bonus, free transport, medical facilities, it also gave employees various benefits like provident fund, insurance, library, sports. Hence it was able keep the employees happy and maintain good relationship.

 "'This is not only "humane", it is also realistic. If your workers are not happy, they are not going to work well. "Larsen commented.

L&T ranks "First" in infrastructure in Business world's survey of India Most Respected Companies and has remained in the rank of top ten companies of India.

Similarly, when L&T grew, with complete factory set up, Larsen was serious about training the persons employed with company, based on division of labour and specialization, then delegating responsibility to manage the show, he believed it was easy to get finance and material for the company but most important part was execution of the job, hence it was necessary to find right persons and then train them in the company before handing over responsibility. L&T managed complete project from design to finish products. It also designed, manufactured or modified products or machinery as per collaborations with other companies, to make them suitable for local needs. Thus promoted" made in India label" took pride of its creativity.

In December 1950 L&T became a public limited company with limited liability.

Larsen's emphasis was on free and fair recruitment policy and then training the staff and workers, observing their performance and then delegating responsibility to manage the show. Managers are made responsible for the work, that's how the company can grow and make its name. He also believed that company can get money and buy materials for the projects, but executing them is difficult, hence trained managers or experienced people are needed to do the jobs. Hence internal staff must to gain experience by executing different projects.

 Whenever Larsen lectured on any subject or did the presentation of a project or appreciation of department performance was concerned, he always believed in inserting some humour in his speeches, it becomes interesting, the audience is not bored with the speaker, and pays attention to his lecture, he advice his people working with L&T to do the same.

it made many products/ machineries which were imported previously, it executed vast varieties of diversified projects in dairy, cement, steel, hydroelectric dams, petroleum refineries even nuclear plants with foreign collaboration, it redesigned them and made them suitable for Indian conditions, it saved foreign exchange for the country.

 After getting married in Bombay during the war, he settled here, for work and business he visited many places in India and aboard. After spending many years of his life in Bombay, he could speak Bombay style Hindi and read Urdu, I also read and speak English, Danish, French, German, Norwegian and Swedish.

In India, he had spent five decades and he felt at

home here also.

"I like India, the people, the food and the culture and indeed I am at home here. But I am not at all out of place in Europe. I have relatives there; I am always going there to see collaborators and my daughter studies in London. I fit in there too." Larsen commented.

Changing color of Bombay

When chairman emeritus of L&T, arrived in city of Bombay in December1935, as consultant for Tata group, that desired ~~who wanted~~ to set up three new cement plants in India, with best Danish technology. ~~at that time,~~ It was the best city in East, an island of Good life, well connected by bus and local trains, a well administrated place, with twenty-four hours water and electricity.

He had spent two months here and the recollections of this place, ~~where he spent two months,~~ remained with him. He ~~he~~ was so fascinated by this place that when time came to escape from Nazi's rule, it persuaded him to come back and take refuge here again, then elsewhere.

Larsen and John both loved boating/ sailing, enjoyed swimming, fishing. They always desired to live close the sea, relished cool sea breeze, charm of the coastlines covered with coconuts trees, old villages, fishing, cultivation, land covered with forest, also the hidden beauty of animals and birds found inside it and on the trees. That's why when more building activity came up in Juhu and it became crowded, Larsen's requested for another a guest house at Aksa in Mudh Island, company accepted it and built it at the same place. He loved wild life and as the trustee of World Wild Life fund, in India, he was involved in preserving it,

Best city in East, left to you to judge.

Larsen had spent seven decades of his life here and had seen it all, growth and decay ~~all~~. He had ~~had spent seven decades of his life here,~~ lived in this wonderful city, from 1938 till 2003. When he first came on this island, most of lands consisted of forest, fields, villages, salt pans and mangroves, a wonderful island city that had everything of his interest in creation and nature, since his childhood, he always desired to see all this, in one life time.

He came to this city at the right time, had the opportunity to see and experience Bombay's natural history, a wild paradise. Then more and more lands consumed by housing and the industrial development that took place. He saw the degenerated of its environment, change was required but not in unplanned manner.

This imbalanced _development of industries_ in India, he though, it was due some states were unable to provide power and better infrastructure, hence they were still in darkness. Which allowed concentration of investment and industries the western region of India, hence the inflow people to find employment and business opportunity here, this city became overcrowded and could not support extra population.

At last, he knew it was also spoilt, by power hungry greedy politicians, due to which government administration became loose, vote bank politics allowed anyone could built a hut on open land (government or private) and claim its ownership. He regretted that Bombay will never recover to its old charm and glory.

Imitating the English man.

Mahatma first imitated the English man's language, dress and ethics, then he gave up, to fight for India's freedom. After long struggle, when it had achieved independence in 1947, he was not power hungry, so became an ordinary Indian but did not live to enjoy the fruits of his efforts.

Mahatma failed to imitate the English man properly and gave up. Nehru educated in England, adopted the same English parliamentary system of governance for India.
Before 1947 India was divided into three hundred and fifty or more independent kingdoms, ruled by kings, nawabs, with diversity of culture, religions, and people spoke more than four hundred different languages, it became one nation with written constitution based on equality and justice.
In1957 the kingdoms were merged into different states based on language; the people spoke.
 English parliamentary system was new form of governance for Indian people, still they adopted it soon, an election system supervised by election commissioner came into existence, an a candidate who secured more votes than his opponent, was declared the winner. This system was of winning election is based on Quantity and not quality. The candidates needed large sum of money first to fight election, it became business type. The candidate first invested huge money, either from the political party or businessman, after winning the election, the

expected elected candidate must make money and return their money back. After winning the election, candidate is expected to make multiple money and to pay back. This greed changed the character of the elected representatives, so elected leaders demanded their pound of flesh before approving the project, corruption crop in, government servants also demanded their cut and became narrow minded and selfish.

The Second World War compelled them to leave their native country and take refuge, now controlled by Nazis, both were similar with Bombay, a safe place, far from the real action of the war, so they settled here.

Destiny had other plans for them, it brought them here to struggle and to make a new beginning. It was not easy to succeed but they were fortunate, to meet two right men with good qualification and experience at the right time that helped L&T, John helped them to find work with port trust, and it survived the most difficult time of Second World War.

As L&T, being qualified engineers did not believe in wasting Time and Talent for mad Hitler who had pride with wrong ideas of capturing whole Europe. They devoted time to different types of civil mechanical electrical instrumentation projects, L&T manufactured and fabrication of heavy machinery for dairy cement helped India's industrial development. L&T had gained experienced in many different fields of engineering, fabrication and manufacturing, it diversified, L&T set up design departments and employed many engineers, designs large and heavy engineering products, precision machineries, spares for need for nuclear plants, like pressure vessels, heat exchangers, calandrias etc and fabricates it.

Now L&T was the big brother and ECC (engineering construction corporation ltd) born before L&T in 1944 considered herself as small sister, she always cooperated and supported her big brother in construction and executing of the projects. Big brother and small sister secured orders cooperated and executed them.

Old friends

1936 Larsen had secured a big contract for F.L.Smidth, Denmark, from Tata group for three new cement plants, but Hitler banned exports, and these plants were diverted to Germany.

His company could not fulfil this contract, was helpless, he still maintained contacts with ACC house at Churchgate, Bombay, and had many Parsee friends in the city, some also worked with the L&T. Through them he was introduced to Dr Homi Bhabha, chairman of atomic energy commission. Who visited Powai works, saw the set up, it had engineers, modern design room heavy fabrication and ECC did completely contract job?

In 1960 L&T & ECC both combined and secured order to build India first nuclear plant in collaboration with other foreign firms, at Trombay in Bombay.

L&T did civil mechanical as per its expertise and constructed it.

Import substitute

L&T executed vast varieties of diversified projects in dairy, cement, steel, hydroelectric dams, petroleum refineries etc. It designed the whole project or invited technical collaboration, manufactured or modified products thus made them suitable for Indian condition which were previously imported, saved foreign exchange for the country.

Nature

He loved God's creation and always eager to travel and see new places or new environment with different natural surroundings and creatures that lived there, for him since childhood it was a way of learning and it broaden his mind. All three founding members were not greedy or attached to wealth, Larsen in charge of the company as chairmen did not take advantage of his position or become a rogue promotor to corner the profits, hence he did not hold substantial ownership in the company, just a marginal stake — about 1.5 per cent. Still, since beginning, he believed it's his own money that is invested in the company, and must earn returns, to repay loans taken from banks, material supplied by suppliers must be paid, wages of workers must be paid in time and not betrayed, or run away with it. Hence, he was trusted by workers and suppliers, that's how L&T built trust and reputation; it is managed by good persons. Since both were open minded and regarded this established their own family or extended joint Hindu undivided family ruled by two Kartas who regarded profit earned must be utilized for welfare of all. L&T provided good salary plus benefits, food canteens, medical, sports, library facilities. Managed on democratic principles open to resolving disputes and differences by peaceful means.

Destiny

1936 Destiny had other plans in its mind, when Nazi invaded Denmark and misruled it, when rape, murder, discrimination was common, which compelled them to leave it. It brought them to Bombay, a safe place, far from the real action of the war, they came here to settle temporary, it was during exile in Bombay, they struggled like other refugees here, fortunately they were joined by veteran experienced project engineer.

It survivesd the most difficult time of Second World War.

As L&T, being qualified engineers, both were with similar experience in setting up cement plant, they did not believe in wasting Time and Talent for the war which they thought, it was madness. They devoted time to different types of civil, mechanical, electrical and instrumentation projects. L&T acted as consultant for dairy, cement brewery, manufactured and fabrication of heavy machinery/plants which helped India's industrial development. L&T had gained experienced in many different fields of engineering, fabrication and manufacturing, it diversified, L&T set up design departments and employed many engineers, designs large and heavy engineering products, precision machineries, spares for need for nuclear plants, like pressure vessels, heat exchangers, calandrias etc and fabricates it.

ECC (engineering construction corporation ltd) born in 1944 before L&T as a limited liability company, it persuaded better returns in manufacturing activities and diversified company, it became a Big brother and supported ECC with projects. During the fifties, ECC remained as a small sister executing big brother dreams. L&T secured and designed projects while ECC constructed and executed them, some of most famous projects that India needed to fulfil electricity shortage, like the India first nuclear atomic reactor plant, ECC did the construction in 1964 at Trombay in Bombay.

Friendship

Larsen and Toubro both went to same school got acquainted and develop trust, after spending many years in school education, they joined the same company. So, it became like a

 long lasting marriage.

 Partnership was based on friendship, understanding and cooperation. From the beginning, each partner was sincere, discipline, hardworking and honest, they realized for good team work is necessary ,for this company to continue and survive, partners must believe and trust each other, this translated into action, thus they alternated role of chairman among themselves. For particular period of time, when one partner was ill or went to perform a job elsewhere or do some consultation work, he could easy leave the responsibility other partner. They cooperated shared the responsibilities of this company equally, when Larsen was absent, Toubro took it over easily, without fear of mischief for he had full trust in his friendship that the other partner will not betray him, similar with the work, how this company functions. They were flexible and believed in democracy, for they always debated before execution of the job.

 ” Time,” was the most precious commodity of their life, not to be wasted but utilize it carefully, given jobs must be completed on time, promised appointments must be honoured in time. For seven long years they were in exile, had lived in Bombay continuously, experience the different climatic conditions of this place. How the clouds cried and shouted, when they collided with each other, which resulted in heavy rains, continuously for two or three days, the roads and railway lines were flooded, buses and trains stopped, were flooded, and life came to stand still, without workers reporting to work, it affected work schedule and routine work disrupted, delayed execution. They decided monsoon season was right time to take leave, alternately during this season they went to native place Denmark and also visited other European countries, spend their holidays there. It was during this period; they also completed the follow up work with other associated companies.

Friends during Bad times

When in exile L&T thought, precious time of our life, must not be wasted, do something creative, in our line of expertise, India is underdeveloped nation and huge place, offers vast opportunities, the engineers, they thought.

So, in 1938 started a partnership firm in Bombay. Within one year setting up, this small unknown firm called L&T, in 1939, Britain declared war on

Germany, it was war time and for many entrepreneurs, it might not be right time, to take risk, what alternate was left for technical qualified refugees, except to struggle on this island.

"Luck favours the brave and courageous persons who take the opportunity when it comes."

In 1942 when imports of dairy machinery stopped L&T did not lose hope, it built self-confidence that it could manufacture same dairy machinery substitutes here, which it imported from aboard.

L&T' first started with one table space only room at Calicut Street, Bombay, it was without design room, fabrication workshop etc, still it persuaded John to do drafting work at Naval workshop, then with help of local workshops it manufactured them here, India first dairy machinery substitutes, supplied them to the British army, they worked as accepted quality product.

1943 It quoted for the naval contract and with help from John, working with Royal navy,

to make merchant ships defend themselves, got it in hand and it survived.

When this work in progress was carried within dock area. On 12 April 1944 freighter SS Fort Stikine arrived at Bombay from Karachi, and when the inferno started in the afternoon, the founding team of four men was present there, God saved them for He had better plan in mind for India and its people.

Secret of a Humble beginning

Fact that L&T was conceived and born in Bombay and had spent its childhood here, by trial and error it survived, experimenting with different ideas.

All this information is always suppressed from the public, it was the same, during its IPO public issue1950

It was less known, L&T is an Indian company, first located in Bombay it provided and still provides jobs and work for Indians. It's an engineering company which has kept on updating its knowledge and skill as per times. Even when engineering education and engineers were not available, it kept on updating its knowledge and skills.

 At present it's a registered public limited company with more than twenty-five thousand shareholders, ninety-eight percent are Indians, its more diversified company, specialized in different fields of engineering, manufacturing, heavy fabrication, in different sectors of different industries. It provides direct employment to more than ten thousand persons and indirectly to lakhs persons and to large group of all type of suppliers.

Soren K Toubro

William Bendictson and John A Gonsalves always worked hard without caring for the rewards or money, they followed Bhagavat Gita.

" Be active don't be inactive, do not react to the outcome of the work"

They had put this small firm on strong footing and after the Second World War, William left it.

1950 when "L&T became public limited company, Soren K Toubro alternated as director and chairman of the company upto1963, he still continued as director on L&T's group of companies, till March 27, 1981.

Since 1938 he, stood as a strong pillar of firm foundation that stood many types of vibration of a strong earthquake. He was humble and encouraged Larsen, they made a humble beginning with one table space only, he believed that this small firm can grow and become large diversified company. He always supported and guide his friend not to give up, even during the period of 2nd world war, when consultants were not getting business, he remained with the partnership, and faced more tremors that came along, He dedicated his life for this partnership firm until it became strong. He was like a good wife who

always supported her husband, stood firm during the storm and sickness,

Larsen receives Awards on behalf of all those who helped to make L&T, GREAT.

1968: Henning H Larsen received award from National Association of Danish Enterprise, 1976 he was Consul General for Denmark in Mumbai
In 1977 he received the Ramon Maqsaysay Award for his contribution towards the industrial development of India and for International Understanding, for bringing different countries closer. He gave a speech at the time of receiving this award in Manila.
" The success that came my way in helping to foster the advancement of industrial development of this great country can be attributed to a good deal of luck but mainly to my fortune in working with competent and devoted team. I therefore share this unique honour bestowed on me today with all those

persons with whom I have had the privilege of working in India as well as with the company's collaborators, contacts, customers on all five continents. The honour truly reflects the ideals and spirit of your great departed leader President Ramon Maqsaysay."

"I don't know whether this is deserved or not, but the happiest fringe benefit of my career is that in 46 years, I have come closer to people of different countries and broadened my international understanding, if not theirs."

"I do not have words to express my feelings, my gratitude, for this great honor done to me. It is an honor not only to my adopted country, India where thousands of my Indians coworkers, colleagues and my friends have supported me, in my endeavors over last forty years but to a far way land, of my birth. I believe I am first the citizen of Denmark to have received this prestigious Award. On their behalf I accept this honor to all humility."

.

Henning H Larsen was also presented with many other awards and was knighthood by the Danish Royalty and also received the Christian Xth

Freedom Medal. The Danish government honored him for his work in promoting trade and Danish Indian relationships.   He was also conferred order of the Knight Commander of Dannebrog 1980. He was also Awarded Sir Jehangir Ghandy Medal for Industrial Peace 1989: Appointed Chairman Emeritus of L&T 1999: Felicitated by Bombay Chamber of Commerce & Industry 2000: Honoured by The Confederation of Indian Industry for his 'vision and spirit of entrepreneurship. Honoured by National Gallery of Modern Art as 'a celebrated figure whose contribution has enriched the field of Indian contemporary art'. Receives Chemtech Foundation's Chemical Industry Stalwart Award in 'recognition of outstanding contribution to the process industry' 2001. Presented Life Time Achievement Award from the Bombay Management Association for selfless devotion to the cause of Indian industry 2002.

 Awarded Padma Bhushan for contribution to Indian industry. On receipt of the award, he remarked: "India, my adopted homeland has a special place in my heart. With the Padma Bhushan, I'm happy to realise that I have a place in her heart too. I regard this honour as a tribute to the unique spirit of L&T, and the values it has always stood by: its professionalism, its commitment to quality, and its concern for the entire community of stakeholders".

He was the trustee of Royal Bombay Yacht Club.

Chapter 21

Reincarnation

Exiled

during the second world war, they were stationed in Bombay, for seven years, it was the most difficult time of their life here, they came to know, the people of India are friendly, peace loving, business type, they need guidance. Having travelled to different parts of India, they came to know, it is a diversity country, with many religions, languages, dress and customs, it's like an ancient fashion house, and its changing with time.

After displacement from native land, Larsen had lived in Bombay for six decades, Toubro lived here for three decades, they understood Indian way of life and they got accustomed to it, so they never felt they are foreigners in this country. It made them think India is our second home and they settled here. They also understood Hinduism, it accepts pluralism, each individual's right, gives him the freedom to worship in his god, in his own way, it is more open-minded religion, different from other religions which dislike idle worship.

Larsen worked and devoted, for thirty-nine years of his life for the company, since its inception with only one table space, when there was little hope of this firm, surviving during the 2nd world war, he always assured his partners William Benedictson, S. K. Toubro and John A Gonsalves to hold on, have faith" better tomorrow lies ahead."

When L&T had no place for drawing room, he also told John," there will be hundreds of tables, placed with in L&T factories"'

Larsen retired in 1977 and continued to live in Mumbai, he had many friends in India and a well-known personality, he also believed in reincarnation, soul is spiritual or spirit that it comes from outside into a temporary physical body and leaves it when a person dies. Karma every action has equal and opposite reaction, we have to repay our debts, if not in this life, then in the next incarnation. God is real accountant and bookkeeper, records every transaction of life in Akashic books of all records. He is compassionate and merciful provides every person one or more chance to realise and purify. Hence incarnation is the way of purification, only pure saintly person can stand before God, that's why, he accepted Hindu philosophy of rebirth, body is temporary abode for the soul or spirit, just like clothes need replacement, the soul or spirit departs after death and needs new body and new clothes, hence he accepted cremation, to let matter return to earth and soul to heaven.

Larsen was more than ninety years old and he became thin and weak, was treated at Breach Candy hospital, ~~Mumbai~~ at the age of ninety-six in 2003 he died. As per his will his body was cremated as per the Hindu tradition at the Chandanwadi electric crematorium, at Marine lines, Bombay in July 2003.

He is survived by a daughter, Jeannette Arnold, and she has two children.

Chapter no 22

Habit becomes an obsession

1492 As sailors, Portuguese landed on the west coast of India., first Kerala, Goa and then Bombay, it was previously ruled by Portuguese and then English. They came as bachelors, married the local women, ~~and Portuguese, came as sailors and married the local women,~~ the missionsy converted the locals to Christianity and mix population prevailed here, they left a common custom among Indian Catholic people, to serve drinks, on occasion of marriage, feast or birthdays.

John joined the crowd during these celebrations and got accustom to social drinking, first, he drank alcohol occasionally and was comfortable with it for many years. Then on weekends, a group of his friends accompanied John and had get together at an old bungalow, where they spent their time together talking, debating and eating and drinking. Gradually it became daily, in the evening his friends gathered in a separate room of another bungalow, He loved to sing and played mouth organ well and carried it with him, his friends brought in other musical instruments, they joined the band, together they played and party went on for two or more hours.

He was earning well and could afford entertaining his friends, encouraged by friends, it became a routine, at first, he drank less he was able to control the devil and after few drinks was in his senses, he could walk properly. Sometimes he crossed his consumption limit, he loss self-control and the devil took over, he was not able to walk properly, somehow managed to find his home. Eunice his wife caught hold of his hand brought him inside house and made him to seat. She brought a piece of ice applied it on his head and gave water to drink, to cool him. The alcohol had captured his mind and the hangover was beyond his control, whatever his wife did to cool his nerves, did not help him much, so he went to sleep without eating.

After 1951 this old habit became an obsession and haunted him, soon he reached the dependent stage. Evening after work, he needed it to cool his nerves that carved for it, soon he realized it had an upper hand on him. Alcohol(devi) was in command of his life, and he had been in its bondage for some years, like a slave to his master.

Now this habit turned into obsession and was beyond his self-control, every time he resolved to give it up, the devil stood close to him, led him to the bottle, he failed to understand, why? He was so addict to it and what tempted him to drink again in the evening? Why he could not remain without drinking alcohol?

Many times, whenever he got drunk, he loses his memory, forgets and misplaces things, he always loss something like his purse, his bag or forgot to collect the remaining change money from the bar owner. Sometimes his hangover lasted until the next morning; and he felt, today he is not in position to attend his duty; he was compelled to take an off. At last, he realized this disease is irreversible, and he is helpless. excessive drinking had led him to the bottom pit of alcoholism. He was searching for an answer, what made him lose his self-control?

What is the cure for this disease? In the morning he prayed and asked god for help to find a way out his drinking obsession. His wife Eunice daily devoted one hour in pray for his sobriety. She had four (sons) children to manage and his recovery was important if not, he may lose his job. After marriage, she had given up a secured well-paying job with a well-established company and became a housewife.

1955

Those days L&T's annual day was celebrated at Bandra Gymkhana, since it was not a large gathering like it is today, a get to gather attended by the staff, workers, both the founders took this opportunity to meet people who worked for the company and then interacted with them.

An engineer promised John, he will meet him at his residence in Bandra and both will attend this party together. This man carried his own stuff with him and came home, so they both shared this stuff at John's home, before attending this function.

Then they attended the party, joked and enjoyed with their colleagues, here again, other types of drinks were served, this cocktails soon turned John's head off that he felt heavy, soon he excused himself and found he could not walk properly, somehow went to the toilet and omitted. Now he felt like resting, so he avoided the crowd, found a lonely corner where he was seated and then went to sleep.

Toubro fond of John wondered where he is? Not to be seen with the crowd present in the hall, so he went in search of him. At last, he noticed him sleeping in one corner; he spoke to him then understood John is drunk, so he did not disturb him but left him to cool down.

John realized his weakness that his addiction has become a cause of his disgrace, it was shameful thing for his boss Toubro to discover it, same problem was also a reason of dispute with his wife, family members and others. I must avoid such type of cocktails or limit my drinking, best thing give it up and become sober.

Two accidents, experiences of his life made him realize, when drunk he could not walk properly or control himself, while crossing the road, accidents most likely to happen hit by a car, or when travelling by the local train he loss his balance and fall, lose his life.

God had saved him and given him new life twice in the past, without God's help he would never be alive. Now he assured himself, no more getting drunk again but he failed sometimes.

He had great faith in God and believed in His assistance he can overcome this problem, he prayed and believed in God existence as controller of this universe, he takes care of all his living beings.

John also knew both good and evil existed side by side, just like particle and anti-particle. Both positive and negative forces also existed side by side, a coin two sides, a person has dual personality. Some persons had experienced evil spirit or seen ghost in some ways or the other in their life, others who did not have this experience, will never believe in the existence of spirit.

When electricity was in its infant stage in Bombay and many places were still not connected to the grid, lights were only in urban areas of main island city. In the village or the suburbs power supply was cut off suddenly. When area from Bandra to Andheri, consist of fields and marshes lands, forest, etc.

During those days, after 7pm till the cock crows at 5am, it is devil time, many have experienced and related their tale to others. A person walked alone on the road, without lantern or no street lights, no one accompany that time the devil crop in misguided him or harmed him and even appeared before him and horrible appearance, made the person insane.

Once late night, John was returning home to Bandra from Khar through the fields. He saw the ghost a scare face personality while walking alone on Turner road since his mind was free and without fear he could bear it.

His mother had a field next to Bandra talkies and she cultivated vegetables. Next incident happened, while walking along same road, he saw big two hulks boxing each other, thinks of stopping this fight, their strange appearances and odd voices, cautioned him, undaunted he watches the show, he moves on, from the other side of the road, far away. Then he understood that it was real ghost or spirit of person, that haunted this place, but now seem like it is an illusion.

Those days the elders who had similar experience of apparitions, warned him, do not be afraid or fear or panic, they cautioned him never look back, once you turn your head, see the horrible real actual scene, person with this experience, many persons have died after they had seen it.

Apparitions are only one side of the coin for many people who have not seen the ghost or had such type of experience. Hence, they did not believe in existence of evil spirit, these things are spiritual type that cannot be proved or experimented to show someone it is real. Hence there are two type of people, the elders said one type who will die without experience of the other side of the coin. But those who had experienced or seen the evil spirit once or twice in his life they know God(good) and evil(devil) both exist, just a coin with two sides or like person with dual personality, that was the difference with person had gone through it.

These incidents, were his real personal experiences of life which proved to him that the devil also existed and he believed it. The devil played important role of tempting man and weakening his self-control, this compulsion to drink, had made him slave to his vice.

At last man become so weak and helpless that God alone could help him and make him understand his weakness, 1956 John hit the bottom and it made him realize god can restore his serenity. He became serious, eager to find a way out of this obsession, resolved to give up alcohol, since it affected his job and his family life.

On day while browsing the newspaper, he came across a small advertisement in in miscellaneous columns, it began with a slogan.

" If you want to drink, that's your business.

If you want to stop that's our business."

This advertisement was put by a foreigner on a visit to Bombay with contact address of a hotel where he was staying at present, visiting timing was mentioned in it. John read it twice or thrice and wondered, "what is this man saying he can stop or show how to give this drinking habit, how he can cure my disease? Or he is just taking some for a ride?

 Would his method be effective or he is just fooling?

For what purpose he has come to Bombay? Many questions roamed in his mind.

" Let me meet him and try." he said to self.

 Next day, he visited the hotel at the given address and on time, when he rang the bell of the hotel room; this foreigner opened the door, he was surprise to find another Indian man is also present here.

This foreigner invited him inside and he started to explain, about this new Alcoholic Anonymous method of recovery, "it is spiritual type; it may sound funny to you but it works," he said and continued.

"when man acknowledges his defeat and humbles himself, sincerely asks god for help. God is ever ready to help him, when people surrender their life and will to god, He gives them grace to recover." He added.

John and professor Harry Mathais, both comprehended this foreigner about this new program of recovery how it functions. What are individual requirements to stop this habit, he kept on explaining about AA, he also handed over some the leaflets to them, these leaflets containing the twelve steps and traditions of AA without explanations.

"If you sincerely follow these steps, you will become sober." This tourist assured them, also gave them the address AA New York headquarters. Told them to keep in touch with it, you can order more literature, books from here.

Some AA literature is free, other you will have to pay, they will provide you free literature to spread the AA message or programs to other sufferers.

"We all have some short comings like egos or pride or resentments or want to take revenge on somebody. This program teaches you to give them up "let go and let god," be humble, God will help you to remove these short comings." He concluded.

"This makes you understand the spiritual of life better.
He continued. "When case becomes hopeless, only god can help a man get relief."
Like you many persons have suffered from alcohol illness and by following this AA program they have recovered in USA." The foreigner concluded.

John was immediately hit on the head by these explanations, thinking this method has the real solution for his problem but it sounds funny,

"How can I surrender my Ego," John said to self.

 "But that was it; you have put principles before personality to recover." He explained.
 Before attending this meeting, Harry Mathais had already read some articles about Alcoholic Anonymous (AA) in Reader digest, it is a fellowship of men and women who share their personal experience with each other, to solve their common problem, to give up drinking and stay sober, then continue to spread the message, to help others

suffering from this disease.

"Main purpose of AA is to spread the message to people suffering from alcoholism, thus help them to recover from this disease."

Harry and John were suffering from the same disease or had similar problems and wanted to give up drinks.

They had further discussion about this method of recovery with this foreigner who advised and assured them that this is simple and reliable method, many people have become sober in USA by following it.

When this session got over, both came out of the hotel and introduced themselves. Harry said he is a teacher and is staying in Mahim Bombay, John a draftsman, works for an engineering company L&T and both exchanged their home addresses. Harry promised to visit John's place and explain this method further.

Chapter No 23

Serenity

In the early 1930s, a well-to-do Rhode Islander, Rowland H. had hit the bottom and found alcohol had upper hand over him and he was a slave to it. He attends the Oxford Group which practiced a formula of self-improvement by taking stock of a person's life or self-inventory, admitting wrongs, making amends where ever possible, using prayer and meditation to improve self-control and get sober or become a better human being. They also shared their personal experience and this method of self-improvement to others.

 Rowland H introduced Vermonter Edwin ("Ebby") to this group, he and others admitted their short comings, became sober by practicing these principles.

Ebby told his story to his school friend Bill W, how he gave up drinking and had sobered now by practicing Oxford Group method of self-improvement and desired to carry this message of hope to other suffers.

At first Bill was skeptic and did not believe in his friend's story of becoming sober through this method.

Bill W' was a successful stockbroker, his career was ruined by continuous drinking, his illness became hopeless and irreversible. Bill at the age of 39 years, he had taken medical treatment at Towns Hospital in Manhattan NY to become sober, he improved a little but then devil is not far, he tempted him again, started to drink alcohol again.

 In December 1934 he was again admitted to Towns hospital for treatment, he realized medical treatment only cannot restore his sobriety, God's help is also essential. Only with God grace a person can become full sober and find peace, so he submitted his life and will in god's hand and practiced the method of self-improvement, he stopped drinking and found peace. Soon He understood this message and the importance of sharing personal experience with other alcoholics. It is essential not only for recovery but also for staying sober.

On Mother's Day, May 12, 1935 Bill relates his story to Dr. Bob who shares his own story with him.

Hours later, Dr. Bob realizes how much spiritual support can come as the result of one alcoholic talking to another alcoholic. Dr. Bob lapses into drinking again but quickly recovers by god grace. June 10, 1935 is known as the date of Dr. Bob's last drink and is also celebrated as the founding date of Alcoholics Anonymous.

Dr. Bob and Bill spend time discussing alcoholism, noted this trial error method of recovery and the principles followed by them sincerely, they noted essential steps taken for recovery and sharing of personal experience.

Realized "Today" is most important day in the life of an alcoholic, to this change his thinking and make him sober. It is very essential, for an alcoholic to live in the present, just for today and follows the twenty-four-hour concept.

"Easy does it, one day at a time."

Yesterday is gone and all the money or gold will not bring it back, tomorrow is suspense and unpredictable, uncertainty is part of life.

 So, if you want to become sober, live for the day" Today."

Now this foreigner had sowed the first seeds of recovery in the minds of two persons Harry M and John G in Bombay and had left it to them to spread the message of Alcoholics Anonymous to other suffers. He had told them, to practicing these AA twelve steps and twelve traditions in daily life is important, he assured them it really works and there are many examples of persons in USA who followed this AA method and became sober.

Those days, very few people knew about AA or even if someone had read about AA in Reader Digest, no one cared to spread the message of AA to others fellow suffers. As they felt it is beyond their self-respect or dignity to speak to a drunkard and a hopeless person who would ignore your lectures, an alcoholic the society thought was beyond repairs or recovery, so it treated them as outcast, just like the untouchables were considered by higher caste persons, due the traditions followed by their caste. There were few persons like Mahatma Gandhi who took a different view and understood them better and offered help, then fought against this discrimination. That's why, the response to this foreigner's advertisement was very poor, there were only two persons, Harry and John who had attended this first AA meeting in Bombay or perhaps in India and these two persons never boosted about it, as being first and were not proud about it, for they knew pride would not help in their recovery.

On a Sunday Harry M visited John G at his home in Bandra, with AA in his mind that sharing of personal experience helps in recovery.

But no human being is perfect or without sin and vice is part of life. Man is like a coin with two sides, a split personality like Dr Jekyll and Mr Hide.

Harry had already started to adopt the AA method of recovery; he practices twelve steps and the work in progress to become sober is on. He knew Sobriety means sharing your personal experience with other suffers thus make them understand AA method of recovery better.

He started to explain AA method of recovery to John

further.

"First step is to admit you are powerless (helpless) over alcohol, second step you came to understand and believe that there is power above all, that wants a person to admit his weakness, become humble and sincere, then only God can pour His grace and restore your serenity, third, you must decide and fully surrender your life and your will, to the Will of God."

He had just explained the first three steps of AA.

 At first John had doubts about this method of recovery.

 "What is this man talking?" He said to self.

"Man must surrender his life and will to god, something odd." He said to self.

John had a long discussion with Harry and gradually he understood this program was something extraordinary, god loved humble and sincere person, who has the willingness give up his pride (ego) and put his trust in Him (i. e. surrender your will and life in his hand). Once man showed his helplessness and humbled himself, god showed him the way to recover. God gave grace and the real spiritual knowledge to men of His choice like the first followers of Jesus Christ.

"By chance this spiritual knowledge has come to me." John said to self.

Jesus said" I praise you Father Lord of heaven and earth, because you have hidden these things from wise and learned, and revealed these things to little children." Mathew, chapter 11 verse 26.

   John read the Gospel regularly, so he soon understood the program and took it seriously. He had suffered a lot due to compulsive drinking and hoped god would one day show the way and give real knowledge, make him sober.

"This spiritual method must be adopted and followed." He said to self again.

So, first thing in the morning, every day after bath, he daily prayed to God, asked His help, to remain sober for just one day,

"Today."

"One day at time, easy does it."

John took the AA method of recovery seriously, soon wrote to AA New York head Office and got response them with some free literature, after that he ordered three sets of books, like12 steps and 12 traditions, the Big of AA, 24 hours a day. These three sets of books were treated as bibles of AA, like ten commandments which he read them regularly, first thing in the morning to understand the AA program better and to get god's grace.

On his reading table stood a USA made gold-plated frame with the pray mentioned enclosed in it,

" God grant me the sincerity to accept the things I cannot changed, courage to change the things I can and wisdom to know the difference."

Daily first thing in the morning he prayed to god, to give him the grace he needs, to avoid the first drink today, thus help him to remain sober for today. Without god help, he may not be able have self-control and fall into same trap, he may go back to same stage from where he has sobered up little for some time.

He kept in touch with the AA head office in New York and regularly received the literature on AA, and then distributed it to other members, to spread the AA message in India. Both Harry and John became serious and devoted their evenings and holidays to spread this message of AA, first to friends and contacts.

Then they felt," we needed a regular meeting place," so they approached the priest of St Michael School, Mahim in Bombay and explained the AA program to him, who was surprise to hear something similar to

Christian faith, trust in god and surrender your will and life to him. This priest quickly understood that alcohol addiction affected the Christian community more, due to which many men suffered and it affected their family income.

If the main earning member had lost his self-control, became helpless, thus lost his job. So, the priests allowed them to use a classroom of the school as meeting place in the evening only. Again, to attract more people, they contributed money and put a similar advertisement in the newspaper.

 "If you want drink that's your business,

   If you want stop that our business."

In this advertisement they mentioned the AA meeting time and the address of this school.

 Initially the response was very poor; few people were willing to try AA's method of recovery. Those days many people desired to become sober but had different opinions, about persons who claimed they had a cure, they thought them as con men that told lies took money and appeared, and these methods did not work for them.

So, few first started to attend these meeting, John or Harry explained the recovery method, that if you sincerely followed the 12 steps and 12 traditions you could become sober.

After attending these meetings and hearing them, some were not willing to admit defeat, some found it difficult to suppress ego, others were not honest with self, so they hit the bottle again. Some found it odd to move in company of people whom the society had declared as "Failures."

But John and Harry did not care what society thought about them, they persisted we must preach that AA is simple method that depends on person self-reliance to improve his short comings, relationship with god and his grace. It is free and there are no club membership charges, no dress code or keeping up appearances, best way is of admitting your defeat, become humble, pray for God's help, by God grace, many have given up drinks and become sober.

Some from Byculla, other places in Bombay, responded to the advertisement and attends the AA meeting at Mahim regularly.

Some were willing to listen; others attended few AA meeting and then disappeared. Some had willingness to follow this program but were not sincere in following it, so they hit the bottle again. The flesh was weak and the devil was not far from them.

"But with some encouragement to give up first drink and remain sober for today was needed." They thought, when a person fails to maintain the sobriety, he should admit or confess his short comings and again ask for god's grace.

By taking stock of your short comings and making amends wherever it is possible, something different people may not like it, to go the person whom he has harmed or cheated previously and say sorry or repay the loan taken.

 Initially people did not trust this method and were not willing to give it a try, unless they were persuaded by others. Harry and John were serious and sincere; persuaded the new comers to attend meetings. When you fail admit your short coming, try again, prayed to god and ask for help; god is always willing to shower grace and show the way. Ask God and you will receive His grace, knock on the door and it will open and He will show the way, make you strong.

They explained to new comers. there was nothing to lose; no one is asking you a favor or money, its voluntary contribution, you give or do not give for AA group, no one will send you out of the meeting or question for non-contribution. It is a nonprofit organization and free, no admission fee or club membership charges are to be paid by any member, no hard and fast rules, no dress code. Only requirement is to admit you are powerless over alcohol and god will do the rest.

Initial two or three times a week, meetings were held in the evening at St Michael School Mahim, they received new comers and explain this program to them, later they also visited some suffers at their homes to explain this program further, many stopped attending, after the first meeting, so lots of persuasion was needed. That encouragement came from first group members who told them to practice AA principles it works. Sometimes the kindness shown by first members was exploited, as some alcoholics were jobless, extracted money from members.

 For those who were not sincere or stubborn, for them it was difficult to follow AA and give up this obsession. Those who realized and followed this program sincerely, developed self-control and overcome this habit became sober, they all stood as stepping stones to success. More started to attend meeting and followed their examples.

Others were emotional attached to the alcoholic way

of life; it took lot of time to sober up.

How to make more people follow this program? This question remained unanswered.

As time went by, people started to attend meetings twice or three times a week. After some elapses, both Harry and John became sober in 1958.They knew if they want to stay sober they must serve others suffering from similar problem. John was more devoted to AA he spent his own money and purchased new books, on correspondence postage expense with New York head office and other places. During the meetings members exchanged their personal experience and the message AA gradually spread to other suffers.

 Now a man from Pali village Bandra was also attending AA meetings at St Michael School Mahim, so someone suggested.

"Why not you two start AA meetings in Bandra?"
It strikes John "why go far to Mahim to attend AA meetings, why not start it in Bandra?"
He thought it will be convenient and close for us, so he discussed this plan with the man from Pali village who agreed.

 They approached the priest of St Theresa church Bandra and explained this program to him, gave the leaflets containing twelve steps and traditions, this priest soon understood that the Christian community needs the service of AA and gave them permission to use a classroom in the evening only. The Pali evening group was established at St Theresa School in 1959. Initial John had collected many articles on sobriety, from Big book and local stories, himself published and printed an AA magazine for Pali evening group, containing articles of interest for new comers and he distributed it free to whos who attended AA meetings, later he could not afford it hence discontinued it.

As AA became known as method of recovery, some ladies came and stood near the door of John's house, requesting him,

"Make my husband sober," forgetting that sobriety depended on the individual self-realization and transformation on God grace.

Many people believed AA program is like medical treatment, easy to make a person sober and wanted a quick solution.

He guided them to attend AA meetings and follow the program sincerely. But they don't realize it is different, it is a self-conversion that fully depends on individual realization that he is helpless, humbles himself and sincerely desires God's help, follows AA 12 steps and 12 traditions. God helps those who help themselves.

Many times, he faced odd situations when consoling and convincing people, especially ladies became difficult, that individual had to take his own initiative, step by step follow AA program first and then God acted through him and created a change in his personality or miracle.

Chapter no 24

Fifty years of John's sobriety

1960

As time went on, gradually AA message spread from Mahim to Bandra, Byculla and other suburbs of Bombay, ~~like Byculla and~~ the membership increased. The message of AA program spread more by word of mouth, more people received AA literature, free printed leaflets and then brought books about AA philosophy, the AA knowledge was books were distributed at meetings, people became aware, this method of cure is something new, worth trying, it works for habitual drinkers, if you follow this program these12 steps and12 traditions give up their habit or alcohol addiction and become sober and also a better human being. AA is a nonprofit organization of men and women, who have come together. ~~Its only purpose is~~ to spread the message of AA to persons~~ople~~ suffering from alcoholism and thus help them to become sober and stay sober. Its only purpose is to make suffers understand if they sincerely follow AA 12 steps and 12 traditions, they can reform themselves.

New groups came into existence and invited old members speak and relate their experience to others, so John and Harry and others traveled to different places and shared their experience. Some people looking at them wondered "it is a miracle how these compulsive drinkers gave up."

Daily routine,

John got up 5.30am in the morning, took bath, first thing he did was to pray, ask god for help for today, these 24 hours. Stood on the table,– aa gold coated frame USA made frame,

stood on the table,"God grant me the serenity to accept things I cannot ehnagechange. Courage to change the things I can and Wisdom to know the difference."

He prayed Ddaily he prayed to God give me the strength, to resist the "first drink," temptation for "Today." He received God grace and was able to stay sober, one day at a time.

Now John could not isolate himself from neighborhood, company friends, relatives and especially AA suffers that knocked on his door any time. He knew he had to face the world, could not lock the door and remain inside always.

He had to socialize, that where they offered alcohol, w~~w~~henever he ~~John~~ attended a wedding, feast or party, he insisted, he had stopped drinking alcohol as per doctor advise, so he demanded an alternative like for soda or Dukes ginger ale ~~or sweet drink~~. "Please do not serve~~no~~ alcohol, I have stopped ~~drinking should be served~~," when he commented, his friends and others had a big laugh, it was like a joke. They could not understand a man can change soon, they tried to put the pressure, he remained firmed and did not change his stand, the crowd ~~persistance~~persistence did not change his mind or stand ~~from the crowd did not change his stand~~. ~~T~~they joked and ~~laughted~~laughed at him, ~~but~~ his demand for alternative drink was met~~,~~ ~~h~~He slow consumed it, in front of the gues~~s~~s~~,~~ ~~H~~he was not far away from the merry making crowd~~,~~ ~~persons~~People still requested him "take, please take," he remained firm and unmoved. "It's a miracle," people commented.

 How did this transformation take place? He was now a follower of AA who seriously practiced its principles, especially twelves steps and twelve traditions, he had surrendered his will and life to God's will, by His grace this transformation has taken place. People did not believe it, is ~~real~~ it really~~is~~ true. They thought and continued to observe him. He continued in same manner whe~~nre~~ ever he went for a wedding or some other event.

Now he tried avoid old friends and he knew if went with them, devil would again tempt him to drink. He was ~~One of his famous sweet drink was Dukes ginger ale,~~ ffond of reading, from his small collection of books stored in the wooden show case, he picked one book at time, he started to read, same time he slowly consumed a sweet drink, he was fond Dukes ginger ale, thus he was able to~~it~~ ~~slow and~~ divert~~e~~ his~~d~~ mind to other things.

After work he was engaged in corresponding with AA New York head office or with other AA groups in India, then redistributing literature from USA ~~thus spreading~~thus spreading the message of AA to other suffers in India, by doing work for AA he was able ~~to divert~~to divert his mind and remain sober he also attended AA meeting twice or three a week.

 Eunice his wife wondered how did this change come about and then she understood, "God has heard my prays and created this miracle." Not only she even others his mother brothers also prayed for his recovery and the miracle was in front of them. Harry lived in Mahim but he died soon, an his ambition of spreading the AA message toothers remained. John and other AA members did not give up, they continued to spread AA, message to others.

 From 1960 onwards, John took own initiative to approached the parish priest first, explained the philosophy, gave him some AA literature and was able to convince him more that AA works.

To start the Pali evening group meeting on time, first thing he did, approached the school peon and obtained the key of the allotted classroom, opened it and kept ready, placed AA literature on the table, dust some benches for people to sit.

 He attended regularly the groups meetings, as the meeting started, more discussion happened and AA members to share their own experience how they became sober, when a member had stopped attending AA meeting, after becoming sober or had he lapsed back into the same addiction, they visited him at home, shared his experience, and thus carried the AA message to other suffers.

 Now the principles of AA 12 steps and 12 traditions, became John's gospel,a way of life, for him AA were more important than money or fame and he followed them religiously.

Having worked with the three founders of Larsen & Toubro ltd, William Bendictson, Larsen and Toubro, he did insist with a about post in L&T or more increments. He had seen the progress made by this one table space only, small firm into a biggest engineer firm in India. Now when he L&T's dream had come true, he also saw the reality, factories and sheds laid in many big cities of India and many subsidiaries acquired, with higher profits, material wealth flashed throughout India, name plates and advertisements appeared everywhere.

Inside these L&T offices and factories thousands of staff and workers were seated, in a comfortable environment, it was not like 1942 at the time of John's first interview, the two founders Larsen and Toubro stood outside their one room rented office, when William Bendictson was seated inside.

It's a mad, mad world, thousands of professional applications for single post, the mad rush of the managements or engineering professionals to get interview or job in this company, he thought it was all vanity fair.

Then to keep William and John happy and stick with

L&T, Larsen kept on giving assurances, "have faith there will be factories and sheds laid, with hundreds of tables."

 William and John contribution were pushed aside, others took credit for big achievements and big works done, got recognition.

 Now L&T has a big building head office, just located little distance from Nicole street at same place Ballard estate Bombay where it began with one table space. Its office is worth admiring, its most advance technical qualified established company, people dream of joining and working for it.

John like William and Toubro was happy to see Larsen receive hundreds of awards, on their behalf even international Ramon Magsaysay Award. John did not care about Awards, nor he regretted, he was paid less for his contributions.

L&T and its management ignored his contributions, many new comers boosted their name and work, got much paid, fame and money. He remained humble and unknown man for contributions. For him the AA principles of (alcoholic anonymous) 12 Steps 12 Traditions were the Ten commandments of God, to be obeyed in all circumstances and all environments, personality takes the second place or back seat and principles come first.

He sincerely and devotedly practiced the 12 steps and 12 traditions of AA throughout his life, these principles had changed his own personality and kept him sober for fifty years.

On the occasion of twenty years' service award for John, Larsen spoke how John's contribution during the initial stage, had helped this small firm to stand on its own feet and prosper. He serviced L&T for more than thirty-five years.

He was invited to speak to other AA groups which had just opened in other parts of India like Chalisegoa, Nagpur, Mangalore etc. He traveled to other place to encourage habitual drinkers to follow AA new members to give up drinking and for who have loss self-control over alcohol, he told them AA way of life, was the only solution that can help and make a person to stay sober for long time.

 He remained sober for fifty years which no one can believe that AA had created this "Miracle," except his own family members, relatives and followers of AA few believed in this miracle.

In 2008 he was 87 years old and was not able to walk, some from Pali evening group and other members visited him at home, they said," John must celebrate your fifty years of your sobriety," he replied, "No, not necessary."

But some members came home, congratulated him and took some photographs with him and presented a souvenir.

In the morning daily he prayed to God to keep him sober for 24 hours only, he conquered himself, "One day at time, Easy does it." He believed in AA philosophy and in God that He was doing or did for him what no one could ever do, by the grace of god he was able to avoid the devil (alcohol) or the first drink.

In evening, he substituted alcohol with Dukes ginger ale, he died at the age of 88 in June 2009 and was buried at St Andrew Church Bandra where he was baptized.